Ethnographic Museums in Israel

Noam Perry
and Ruth Kark

Ethnographic Museums in Israel

Noam Perry and Ruth Kark

Published by ISRAEL ACADEMIC PRESS, New York

(A subsidiary of MultiEducator, Inc.)

180 E. Prospect Avenue • Mamaroneck, NY 10543

Email: nhkobrin@Israelacademicpress.com

ISBN # 978-1-885881-48-9

© 2017 Israel Academic Press

Photo credits:

p. 87, bottom, courtesy of the Memorial Museum of Hungarian Speaking Jewry. Cover image and all others by Noam Perry. The cover photo depicts a Damascene reception room, from Treasures in the Wall Ethnography Center, Acre, taken Aug. 2008.

To my father, Moshe Perry
who inspired me with love of the Land of Israel,
its history and geography

Table of Contents

Introduction

"There is a passion for museums in Israel, a passion for preserving and interpreting the past" (Rosovsky and Ungerleider-Mayerson, 1989, 6) wrote Nitza Rosovsky, and to a great extent rightly so. In 1983, the Knesset enacted the "Museums Law," which—for the first time in Israel—included a statutory definition for a museum: "A not-for-profit institution that has a collection of exhibits of cultural value, which it displays in whole or in part on permanent exhibit to the public, with the aim of the exhibition being for education, study, or entertainment" (Ministry of Justice). Within the framework of the law, the "Council of Israeli Museums" was established, which is authorized to declare museums "recognized" by the State of Israel. Recognized museums receive state support, and in turn, are required to meet certain criteria as to museum administration, collection methods, handling and care of the collection and its presentation, publication of catalogs, and so on. Today, the State of Israel recognizes 56 museums, most of them devoted to archeology and history. Other prominent groups are: art museums, museums for security-related subjects (the IDF and pre-State military organizations), Holocaust memorial museums, and a few science and nature museums (Rousso, 2004).

In addition, there are many dozens of unrecognized museums. For example, in 1990 Yehudit Inbar and Eli Schiller counted 180 museums plus some 40 local exhibitions, small archeological collections, and museums in stages of formation—a total of about 220 museums (Inbar and Schiller, 1995, 5). Five years later another 22 museums were added, a rate of increase of more than 4 museums a year (!) (Inbar and Schiller, 1995, 268). On the Internet site "Israel

Museums Guide," 219 museums are listed (Israel Museums Guide). Whatever their number, it is rather high in proportion to the size of the population.[1]

The range of topics with which museums in Israel deal is also expanding from year to year, and new types of museums are also being established (for example, open museums and experiential museums), most of them not affiliated with government authorities, but rather at the initiative of individuals or private institutions and owned by them (Schiller, 1990, 246). In the past 30 years many changes have occurred in the thinking about museums and the importance attributed to them. Various universities have opened courses and even entire curricula that deal with museology; journals were even founded in Israel devoted to the field (Lifschitz and Schiller, 1995, 269).

This book focuses on ethnographic museums. Among the museums in Israel, this is a developing category that stands in the shadow of the dominant museum genres and heritage sites in Israel, the large part of which are devoted to the history of Zionist settlement and/or the different types of security institutions. Establishing a museum devoted to one specific Jewish community stresses, in a way, what is different and presents the community as a separate entity. So conceptually, ethnographic museums pose a challenge to the hegemonic Zionist story, which from its outset has been striving to unify the range of Jewish communities under a single ethnic rubric (Kark and Perry, 2008). Yet, as this study shows, in reality most of the communities chose to emphasize their commitment to the Zionist endeavor through the museums they founded.

Research Goals and Methods

Since no comprehensive previous study has been done on ethnographic museums in Israel, this study was carried out as a cross-sectional analysis, with the primary aim being to map the ethnographic museums in Israel. To that end, we decided to use a broad definition, so as to be able to include as many museums as possible. Taking inspiration from the State of Israel's definition above, the term "ethnographic museum" in this study refers to any institution open to the public that displays objects of everyday life from the material culture of the recent past[2] for purposes of education, study, and enjoyment. We availed ourselves, among others, of the following sources in seeking museums that meet this definition: guides to museums and trips (Inbar and Schiller, 1995; Shalev-Khalifa, 2006), online search engines,[3] daily newspapers[4] and colleagues and family members who occasionally provided a lead to unfamiliar places. Ultimately, in this manner, 34 institutions were located that met the criterion.[5]

Part of the museums are veteran institutions, and they are "recognized" according to the definition of the State of Israel, while some were established recently under other names, such as heritage centers or homes. Some of them extend over a number of floors, while others are as small as one exhibit table. Most of them focus on one ethnographic group (community), while others represent a number of communities, one next to the other. While a portion of them have been neglected for lack of budget, a few are garnering ever more interest, and the number of visitors is constantly growing. This is a result of the many guide books for touring, as well as sections on sites to visit that regularly appear in newspapers and deal with the search for small, "unknown" places.

Since, as noted, this is an initial study of its kind, we chose the Grounded Theory research method. This is a qualitative research method, which refrains from forcing an existing theory on the object of the study but rather strives to reach direct conclusions from the information gathered (Charmaz, 2001; Glaser and Strauss, 1967). In line with this research method, this study is inductive in nature and does not aspire to make it fit one or another existing theory. In light of this, the research questions are exploratory in nature, as follows:

- What are the factors that led to the relative rise in the number of ethnographic museums in Israel in recent years?

- What characteristics are common to the ethnographic museums in Israel, and is it possible to assign them to categories? Is it possible to identify a joint narrative history?

- In what ways do the characteristics of the community represented influence the nature of the museum, and in what ways is it influenced by the personality and personal background of the museum's founders?

Most of the information contained in this book was collected through fieldwork of visits to the different museums that were identified. During the visits, Noam Perry documented the exhibits, to the extent possible through photography; there are also semi-structured interviews with the museum founder or its current administrators. Because of the broad view and the large number of museums that were located as early as the beginning of the study, it was impossible to conduct comprehensive interviews with each one of the museums' initiators. So for museums on which research works have already been written, which included in-depth interviews with founders, we relied upon the previous studies, and it was preferable to interview precisely those whose work has not yet been academically studied. The museum visits took place in 2006–2008. In addition to the visits and the interviews, also collected was material previously published on the different museums, produced both by them and by external elements, such as academic articles, the daily press, and Internet sites.

Every research program includes a series of decisions as to the limits of the study in time and space. The first museums in Israel were established in the second half of the nineteenth century, and their development is reviewed briefly in chapter 3. Despite that, this study focuses on museums founded after 1948, for two main reasons. The first, essentially programmatic, is that the establishment of the State of Israel led to extensive changes in the field of museums, as happened in other social and cultural spheres. The second reason, the pragmatic one, is that most of the museums founded before 1948 did not survive, so it is not possible to visit them. Despite that consideration, we chose to refer to museums established after 1948, but not extant today, for purposes of the completeness of the research. Naturally, the discussion on these museums relies mostly on secondary sources, mainly archival information. A review of the first museums in Israel and their historical development is found in chapter 3.

This study relates to all the museums in the State of Israel and the Palestinian Authority. This approach was not taken owing to one or another political stance, but from the idea that as long as there are no official border checkpoints, the museums located beyond the "Green Line" share the space with those within it. Understandably, this choice enriches the study and reinforces its results, especially in light of the link between Palestinian museums on both sides of the "Green Line." Unfortunately, it was not possible to visit museums under Palestine security control, yet a few visits were made to museums over the "Green Line."

Table 1: Museums included in the book, by type of museum

National Museums	5
Museums of Jewish Communities	14
Museums of Arab-Palestinian Communities	5
Museums of Druze, Bedouin, or Circassian Communities	6
Museums of a Location	4
TOTAL	34

The Book's Structure

The book has three parts: chapters 1–3 are introductory. Chapter 1 presents a brief summary of the history of the museum in its various guises over time and focuses on new conceptions of the nature of the museum in light of post-modern theory. Chapter 2 is devoted to the historical development of the ethnographic museums and to the growth of new museum models according to the changes discussed in chapter 1. Chapter 3 reviews the history of museums in Israel, especially the ethnographic museums established before 1948.

The second part of the book, chapters 4–8, presents the findings of the study. The history of each museum is given, while concentrating on the establishment process, the museum's founders and their motivation. Then, the vision of the museum is described, its goals, and the activities organized within its framework. Finally, a concise survey of the museum exhibition is presented. The division into chapters reflects the categorization of the museums according to type.

The third part, chapters 9–10, includes a discussion of the results and a summary. The discussion focuses on the division of the museums into different types and tries to pinpoint the reasons for these differences in factors that motivated the founders of the museums, or in the characteristics of the community that they represent. The summary centers on a number of pivotal issues deserving of further study, such as the relations of the museums with the Zionist movement, their relations with the communities they represent (or claim to represent), and so on.

Chapter 1

ᕙ

The Role of the Museum–
A Modern Institution
in a Post-modern World

Over the course of history, the institution of the museum has gone through many transformations, and the roles it played changed considerably. The beginning of museums dates from ancient times, when kings in the Ancient East consolidated private collections of valuable treasures and loot from war campaigns. In the classical period the term "museon" was formed as the dwelling places of the muses,[6] and a famous institute by this name was founded in Alexandria and functioned as a kind of research institute for leading scientists (Euclid, Archimedes, and others) in their advanced studies. In the Middle Ages, churches and monasteries amassed collections of ritual objects and items of religious importance, thanks in no small part to the Crusades, responsible for the transportation to Europe of many art objects from different places in the world. At the same time, similar collections also began to appear in the Far East. During the Renaissance, wonder-rooms (Wunderkammer) flourished throughout Europe; they belonged to noble families and contained a mixture of art works, unique items from the animal world, and other curiosity stimulating objects (Alexander, 1979, 6–9).

At the end of the seventeenth century, the first university museums were established in Basle (1671) and Oxford (1683), and they began to serve scientists as halls for the presentation of their discoveries in the natural sciences. The explanations appended to the exhibitions were concise and adapted to a limited, highly educated audience of visitors (Alexander, 1979, 9–10). This was the period in which the stereotypical image of the museum, which is prevalent today, was fashioned as a temple of knowledge. In this role, the museum embodies the modernist idea, that it is possible (and necessary) to amass everything (of "value"), to close/hide/sequester the collection in a timeless structure and to arrange it logically and systematically (Foucault, 1986, 26). Gradually, these museums and royal collections began to be opened to visitors. The Louvre in Paris is considered the first national museum, after it came under the aegis of the French Revolution changing from a royal palace to the museum of the republic (1793). By the mid-nineteenth century, in almost every Western country, a national museum or national art gallery had been established (Duncan, 1994, 279). Attesting to their wide distribution in the twentieth century is the fact that in 1904 museums were found in 211 cities in Britain, with 29 of them operating in London itself (Murray, 1904, 292–312).

During the twentieth century, extreme, radical changes occurred in the perception of the role of the museum. As early as 1917, J. C. Dana, the founder of Newark Museum in the United States, argued that the function of the museum had been exhausted as an institution whose purpose was to preserve art works. In his article "The Gloom of the Museum," he criticizes European culture, which had frozen the image of the museum as a temple for works of art, in which the curators are likened to priests. Dana pointed out that the existing museums exclusively served the social elite and were inaccessible to the general public, both physically and intellectually, owing to the realm of content they offered. He noticed the beginning of an era of mass consumption of culture and art and saw that stores, commercial galleries, and industrial plants were becoming more aesthetic and opening their doors to the public and how the public was happily streaming to them. He called for turning the museum into a product for mass consumption that would attract many types of visitors (Dana, 1917).

In 1942, Theodor Low, an educator at the Metropolitan Museum of Art ("The Met") in New York, wrote that the museum must revitalize its educational role and not focus solely on acquiring objects and preserving them. He called upon the authorities to define museums as educational resources in service of the public, alongside schools and universities (Low, 2004, 30–43). Low, who was invited to write about the functions of the museums by the American Association of Museums (AAM), inspired a years-long discussion among the policy makers in the museum world as to the educational role of the museum (Anderson, 2004, 10).

In 1971, the Canadian museologist Duncan Cameron (1971, 11) determined that the main difficulty of museums in his generation was the definition of their identity and role. "Our museums are in desperate need of psychotherapy," he argued, and he diagnosed the situation of the museums as schizophrenic. The source of the problem, in Cameron's opinion, was rooted in the museum's two contradictory social functions: as a temple it should constitute objective, universal, eternal presentation of reality; as a forum, the museum serves as a meeting point for differing approaches—a public arena for cultural confrontation. Cameron (1971, 24) called for the integration of these two roles and argued that if the museum would not realize its function as a forum, its existence as a temple would only act as an obstacle to necessary social changes.

Since then and all through the 1970s and 1980s, as the post-modern and deconstructive discourse and their influences took root, innumerable discussions took place on the essence of the museum. Joseph Noble (1970, 27–32), in time president of the AAM, pithily defined the five activities to which every museum is obliged: collection, conservation, study, exhibition, and communication. Noble compared these five activities to a hand's five fingers: each one is independent but together they serve a common goal. The International Council of Museums (ICOM) held a number of penetrating discussions over the course of the 1970s. These led to a series of crises and ultimately resulted in the following definition: "A museum is a non-profit, permanent institution in the service of society and its development, open to the public, which acquires, conserves, researches, communicates and exhibits the tangible and intangible heritage of humanity and its environment for the purposes of education, study and enjoyment" (Murphy, 2004, 3; ICOM Statutes, Article 3).[7]

In the following two decades, and again in the spirit of postmodernism, the focus of the public and academic discourse shifted to the museum visitors and to the museum as an experiential (rather than educational) institution. Museologists began to wonder why "acquisition" and "conservation" always appear in the various definitions before "communication" and "exhibition"—an allusion to the traditional power structures and passé orders of priority (Murphy, 2004, 3). Museum professionals began to acknowledge the fact that different visitors had various aims in coming to the museum. These aims do not necessarily coincide with those of the museum planners and directors. For example, the most meaningful experience for a certain visitor might be the result of an interaction with another visitor, and not interaction with the exhibit (Veil, 2004, 78). Since then, dozens of studies have tried to understand and examine the visitors' point of view with the aim of improving communication between them and the museum (Hooper-Greenhill, 1994). The leading museums today strive to provide experiences capable of stimulating inspiration among the visitors and to change the way in which they see the world and their lives (Skramstad, 1999, 128).

Today, in the twenty-first century, the digital era and the information revolution create unprecedented political and social changes, and their influence has not bypassed museums and their functioning. The museum has lost part of its prestige as an institution preserving and collecting information for scholars and students, at a time when a tremendous amount of information is available on the Internet. Yet, many museums have made wise use of new technologies, including online means, so as to provide accessibility to their collections to audiences in a way that was previously impossible and even to reinforce the connection with the community they serve (Ballantyne and Uzzell, 2011, 85–92). Museums dealing with cultural heritage are experiencing a more severe crisis. Collecting exhibits, conserving them and presenting them, all require a great deal of resources. The physical establishment of a museum also demands space, which must be paid and cared for. It is much easier and cheaper to create and maintain a website that will support the needs of preserving the collective memory of the community. As Marc Pachter, former director of the Smithsonian's National Museum of American History, has noted, however, there is an emotional component to a museum visit that is not part of a visit to an Internet site. Physical proximity to the exhibits enhances their significance for the visitors (Pachter, 2010, 332–35). This is doubly true when the visitors have a natural emotional tie to the exhibits, as applies to ethnographic museums that preserve the cultural heritage of their community.

Finally, note should be made of the increasing current tendency, also reflected in this study, to consider museums themselves as objects of research. In the past, the museum exclusively served scholars involved with the field it represents. For instance, an archeological museum would serve archeologists and students of archeology to study the subject. Today, an ever-increasing number of scholars in the social sciences make use of the museum to study something about the society in which it grew, each one from the viewpoint of their sphere of knowledge.[8] Museums constitute an informative example of the way in which culture is encoded and made part of the establishment by society and of the manner in which knowledge is bestowed upon the public. In the spirit of postmodernism "The museum itself has turned into a museum exhibit, an item in an archive whose borders have been lost" (Azoulay, 1996, 1–2).

Chapter 2

᪥

Ethnographic Museums—
Historical Roots and Contemporary Trends

While at the outset museums were institutions representing many fields, dealing with anything "worthy" of collection and conservation, over time the museum world underwent a process of "academization." The essence of this process was the division of museums into categories of knowledge, similar to the division into academic disciplines. There began to be museums founded for a specific field: art, natural sciences, archeology, and so on. In each such group, museums began to operate with a link to the parallel scientific discipline, to present its achievements, and to serve its scholars and students. One of the types of museums that developed in this way was the ethnographic museum, which functions with a connection to the academic discipline of anthropology.

A good example of this type of museum is the national ethnological museum in Leyden, Holland, the Rijksmuseum voor Volkenkunde, one of the first museums in the world devoted to ethnography. Its beginnings stem from the Museum Japonicum, established by Philipp Franz von Siebold, a German physician who spent eight years in Japan teaching European medicine and amassing thousands of objects in daily use. When he returned to Europe and began teaching at the University of Leyden, he exhibited them in a museum set up in his home in 1837 (van Gulik, 1989). By the end of the nineteenth century, some twenty similar private museums were scattered throughout Europe and the United States, with their common denominator being the collection and exhibition in Europe of objects found in daily use in faraway cultures, their goal being enabling the European public to be impressed by them while close to home. These museums were nurtured by colonialist concepts, and a large part of their collections were based on items brought to Europe under the aegis of the institutionalized colonization process of Africa (Shelton, 2006, 64–65).

That being the case, the ethnographic museum originally presented cultures located elsewhere. To offer cultures that lived in a former period of time, historical and archeological museums were founded, focusing in the main on the history of the region in which they were established. In other words, the ethnographic museum took the visitors to another place, while the historical museum took them to another time. In contrast to these two types, in recent decades, we increasingly see the establishment of new museums that constitute a combination of the ethnographic and historical museum.

As ethnographic museums, they relate the story of one ethnic group, with a given, distinct cultural heritage. As historical museums, they focus on the characteristics of life as lived in the past in the place where they are located. In part, these museums document and preserve cultures on the verge of extinction, or that have already become extinct, as a result of processes of emigration and assimilation or modernization. Both in these museums, as well as the large establishment museums, emphasis is being shifted from national history toward everyday history of "ordinary people" (Dicks, 2000, 1; Weil, 1999, 229). In the ensuing pages, I will survey a few kinds of such local ethnographic museums, which have become part of the establishment in recent decades in different areas of the world.

2.a. Post-Colonial Museums

As a European creation, museums played a major role during the period of colonialism. In areas that were until recently a target of European imperialism, the new museums were devoted to the local cultures, which had practically been eradicated under colonial rule. Benedict Anderson pointed out that "museumizing" the historical-cultural heritage of native peoples was one of the definite means that colonial regimes used to firmly base their control of their colonies. After the colonial regimes collapsed, the independent countries that were founded in their stead were the unintentional heirs of the mentality of political use of museums and began to exploit them for the creation of national cohesiveness, just like the national museums in Europe (Anderson, 2000, 215–22). National museums were established in the 1970s, in various developing countries, in an attempt by their rulers to outwardly present a façade of a pro-Western liberal regime (Duncan, 1994, 278–80). Conversely, in recent decades, more and more museums have been founded that strive to reconstruct the local culture as it had been before the arrival of "the white man" (Makuvaza, 2002).

As expected, in places in which the native people remained a minority among a majority of European origin, founding new museums was often accompanied by quite a bit of friction. In Australia, an effort was made by people belonging to the museum establishment to create a dialogue with the native aborigines (Kelly, Bartlett, and Gordon, 2002, 14). An example can be seen in the dispute that arose in conjunction with the founding of the National Museum of Australia and what exactly constituted the "Australian nation." A state committee proposed to focus instead on "the continent of Australia." In the end, it was decided to concentrate on the great variety within the "Australian nation," and in particular to highlight the history of the Aborigines.

Despite numerous planning committees, brainstorming groups, and research into what was being done elsewhere in the world, the museum was, during its establishment and after its opening, the object of severe criticism from politicians and many people from the world of culture (Casey, 2006).

In New Zealand, there is tension between the establishment museums and the Maori population, which considers their cultural and art treasures sacred entities that should be respected. Over many years, the museums collected Maori art and ethnographic exhibits, displaying them out of context, which in Maori tradition is considered tasteless and offensive. In an experiment conducted on behalf of the state to bridge this conceptual gap, the Maori leadership was made part of the curatorship, and members of Maori tribes underwent professional training and found their places as workers in establishment museums. At the same time, members of other tribes strove to take absolute control on the way their material culture was to be displayed and interpreted, and they established new museums of their own (Hakiwai, 2005, 157–60).

In both Australia and New Zealand bitter disputes broke out as to the future of human remains, including mummified bodies, skulls, and bones, which had been removed by Western scholars for scientific research. Such remains have already been found for hundreds of years in archeological, natural science, and art museums throughout Europe. In recent decades, as increasing numbers of native societies have gained access to education and legal representation, many have sought the return of ancestral remains for reburial in line with local traditions. With greater sensitivity to this issue, many museums and research institutes have taken steps to return remains, which can sometimes be more than ten thousand years old (Chamberlain, 1994, 60; Jones and

Harris, 1998). At the same time, quite a number of museums today still refuse to relinquish the exhibits in their possession (Sciolino, 2007).

In the United States, tribal museums devoted to Native American heritage are flourishing (Gwyneira, 2005, 3). The establishment of such museums was prompted, first and foremost, by political motives against the backdrop of hundreds of years in which these cultures were presented in natural science museums, making perverted, hurtful use of their ritual objects and even of human remains. This long-term attitude left significant emotional residue which lasts still today in American society, for example, in popular culture relating to native peoples. The founding of museums by these cultural groups enables them to provide their original interpretation to their history, culture, and art (Simpson, 2001, 138).

In Canada, which officially declared its promotion of multiculturalism, in recent decades, numerous debates arose to the manner in which the Canadian museums present the First Nations of Canada. One criticism focused on the fact that contemporary works of art by descendants of natives are classified as ethnographic exhibits, and not as art, so accordingly they are displayed in the Canadian Museum of Civilization and not in the National Gallery of art (Cannizzo, 1991). A similar confrontation took place when one of the museums held an exhibit of the First Nations of Canada with the naïve intention of displaying the wealth and variety of the many native cultures. Yet, it was claimed that items displayed had been obtained through theft, and that the exhibit ignored current burning issues affecting the native population. As if that were not enough, the First Nations exhibition was funded by a corporation drilling for oil on land that had been expropriated from one of the First Nations (Ames, 1992, 139–50).

As a result of the multicultural policy, sincere attempts are being made in Canada to make use of museums in bridging between the different cultures. The museum is perceived as sacred territory in joint public space, which enables gaining unmediated familiarity with "the Other," especially for the majority regarding the minority culture. A few years ago, when an exhibit on First Nations was planned for the Québec Museum of Folk Culture, descendants of these groups took part in preparing the exhibit and guiding it, and it succeeded in uprooting prejudices the visitors held regarding the First Nations (Allan and Anson, 2005, 119–32).

2.b. Museums of Migration and Migrants

Many museums are devoted to migrant groups, whose story is not familiar to the general population of an area. A British study from the 1990s revealed that minority groups almost never visited the many museums in London. In an attempt to attract visitors from minority groups, a number of London museums set up exhibitions presenting a range of cultures. Exhibitions that elaborated upon the experiences of minorities did achieve great success among the migrant public in Britain (Merriman and Poovaya-Smith, 1996). In the United States an increasing number of museums are devoted to African American history and culture (Ruffins, 1992), and recently, to the Latino heritage, inter alia, as an act demanding political recognition of these cultural groups today (Cadaval and Finnegan, 2001; Rios-Bustamente and Marin, 1998, xiii–xvii).

2.c. Commercial-Tourist Museums

Over the course of the past forty years, the entire world has experienced a wave of tourism based on cultural heritage (Heritage Tourism). Under this rubric, more and more museums are coming into being through understanding their potential to attract tourists and draw in income. An example of this is the Ecomuseum type, which was developed in France in the 1970s and gathered impetus throughout Europe and the United States. According to the original concept, this was a holistic museum, presenting to tourists the region in which it is located as an entirety and displayed in it are the complete historical and cultural context of the exhibits in an attempt to link the past to the present (Davis, 1999, 226; Poulot, 1994, 215). Among other things, museums of this type emphasize the human landscape of the space and present the communities that lived within it according to the accepted pattern of ethnographic museums. In distinction from the classical ethnographic museums, the ecomuseum is intended to take into consideration not only the need for preserving the past, but also the present needs of the community, so as to enable it to develop in the future. Yet, despite their good intentions these museums have been criticized as too commercial—seeing their role only as attracting tourists and only pretending to preserve the cultural heritage (Howard, 2002, 69–70, 63–72). Over the years, the term "ecomuseum" was taken out of its original context and adopted by many museums with no commitment to the principles from which it developed (Davis, 1999, 219).

In Eastern Europe a phenomenon developed of refurbishing old installations that had been closed for economic reasons, readying them to receive visitors, and reopening as museums. One example is a salt mine in Slovenia, which restored the original manual production methods, and hope to maintain the museum by selling its products (Rudin, 1995, 26–27). A similar pattern was followed in eastern Canada for museums combining maintenance of local production methods, with marketing their products to its visitors. The commercial element is striking in the name given to them—Economuseums (Herreman, 2006, 423).

2.d. Common Characteristics of the New Types of Museums

Whatever the names and designations given to museums of the new trend, all of them constitute part of that same goal of linking the past to life today and putting greater stress on the people and less on the objects. These museums created a new type of connection with their environment and with the local population, and they have a closeness and intimate acquaintance with the people living the culture they represent. This familiarity enables the museums to become attached to their audiences in a firm, deep manner. One of the advantages is seen in the process of collecting the items. Curators of museums devoted to black culture in the United States revealed that maintaining a sincere, shared connection with the people donating their objects to the museum display allows them to receive not only the items themselves, but also the initial interpretation and the authentic cultural context of those items (Gaither, 1992, 59–62).

In the overwhelming majority of cases, the museums grow from a need of the community and at its initiative, to the point that they are called "Community-Based Museums" (Hoyt, 1996, 90–93). Such a museum has the potential to become a unifying factor for the community during the process of its establishment, and certainly after it opens. It reinforces the self-identity of the community and to a great extent also its self-value. Sometimes the museum even turns into an active participant in the creation of the community and its definition (Karp, 1992, 12; Fuller, 1992, 328). The dialogue with the community can continue during the on-going administration, such that a two-way channel is created for the transmission of information, in which the community nurtures the museum, and not only the opposite (Perin, 1992, 182–83).

Taking a broader view, the new museums herald a change in the social order of priorities and a deflection of the political loci of power. The new model of a museum growing out of the community, and not managed or supervised by the state, presents an antithesis to the old model, modernist in nature, of the national museum. A national museum, by its very definition, participates in the process of creating and defining a united populace around the nation-state. As such it represents a uniform and common past, and erases any remnant of the unique heritage of the different communities found in the society.[9] Thereby, the museum turns the past into a museum exhibit—objective, rational, and distant from the people who experienced it. The local ethnographic museum of the new model constitutes an antithesis to this model. It draws its power from the local knowledge of the people who are creating it, who are not part of the political or cultural establishment. This is part of the democratization process and decentralization of knowledge and the ways of disseminating it, an essentially post-modern, subversive process (Walsh, 1992, 176).

Chapter 3

᠅

History of Museums and Ethnography
in Israel

3.a Roots and Beginnings

The history of museums in Palestine,[10] as in the entire Middle East, is intertwined with the history of European scientific study of the region, which gained impetus in the second half of the nineteenth century. The establishment of the first museum in Jerusalem, and in all of Palestine, is attributed to the British consul in Jerusalem, James Finn, and his wife, Elizabeth Anne Finn. As early as 1849, the Finns founded the Jerusalem Literary Society; the "object of this Society is the investigation and elucidation of any subject of interest, literary or scientific, of any period whatever, within the Holy Land" (Finn, 1878, 91). As part of the society's activity, a small museum was created in one of the consulate's rooms; it contained various antiquities, gifts, and mementos collected by the Finns over the course of their travels throughout Israel as well as different findings sent by British archeologists working in Egypt and Mesopotamia. In the speech he gave on the occasion of the society's establishment, Finn said that men of culture and naturalists in Palestine have an advantage over their European counterparts since they could compare real life as they observed it in their times with the stories of the Old and New Testaments (92–93).

This approach, which sees in scientific research of the "Holy Land" a means for understanding the Holy Scriptures, as well as for proving their faith, led to the founding of other European research societies in Jerusalem, and they, in turn, set up small museums to display their findings. Such museums were established in the second half of the nineteenth century, for example, by the German Der Deutsche Verein zur Erforschung Palästinas (Goren, 1999, 183–87), the French École Biblique (Barkay 1981),[11] and the British Palestine Exploration Fund—PEF, which inherited the Finns' collection after they left Jerusalem (Finn, 1892, 266). Along with this, the collections that had accumulated for hundreds of years in the cellars of the various churches and monasteries in Jerusalem were gradually opened to the public. These included, for instance, the Museum of the Armenian Patriarchate in the St. James Monastery (Schiller, 1981, 24–26); two museums of the Greek-Orthodox Patriarchate: one in the Valley of the Cross Monastery and the other in the Patriarchate's monastery adjacent to the Holy Sepulchre (Tzaferis, 1985); and two museums of the Russian Church (Vilnay, 1970, 273–74; Barkay, 1981, 41).

The founding of new museums was accelerated even more as a result of the "Archeological Excavations Law" enacted by the Ottoman Empire in 1884, which was aimed at coping with the ever-increasing phenomenon of archeological delegations coming from Europe and taking their findings away. The law determined that any archeological finding discovered throughout the empire was the property of the state and had to remain within its bounds and was subordinate to professional inspection by the Imperial Museum in Constantinople (Ben-Arieh, 2000). In 1901, upon the local initiative of Isma'il Bey, head of Public Instruction of the Ottoman rule in Jerusalem, and the British archeologist Frederick Bliss, along with the financing and professional guidance of the Ottoman Hamdi Bey, director of the Imperial Museum, a municipal antiquities museum was founded, which was the first government-owned museum in pre-Mandate Palestine. The museum was located in the government high school, the Rashidiyyah School, in the al-Ma'amuniya complex in the Bab Huta neighborhood, very close to Herod's Gate (Perry, 2007; Vilnay, 1974, 390; Luncz, 1901; Bliss, 1901).[12] The museum instituted a slew of innovations seen for the first time in pre-Mandate Palestine, such as display of exhibits in large glass cabinets, arrangement of exhibitions according to chronological order, and the editing of a catalogue of the exhibits.[13]

3.b. The Beginning of Jewish Ethnography

Simultaneous to the development of museums in Palestine, Jewish communities in Europe began to organize museums about the Jewish people. As early as the 1870s, in Germany and Paris exhibits of Jewish art where held, based on private collections of ritual objects. Flourishing at that time in Europe was a relatively new science that delved into research on the folk culture of European peoples. This science, nurtured by the modernist ideas of nationalism, took on various forms and names in different places: ethnography, ethnology, folklore, and the like (Hasan-Rokem, 1977, 5). In light of this background, interest in Jewish folk culture did not lag far behind. Across Europe, groups of Jewish *Maskilim* banded together; they considered the collection of the treasures of Jewish culture and their preservation and study a means for the development of Jewish historical awareness. As a result of their activity, in 1897 the first Jewish museum in the world was established in Vienna, and following it, up to the end of the first decade of the twentieth century, additional Jewish museums were in Frankfurt, Prague, Budapest, New York, and Warsaw (Kol-Inbar, 1992, 10–11; Itzkowitz, 2006, 8–9).[14]

The man most identified with the development of Jewish ethnography is Shloyme Zanvl Rappoport, known by his pen name

An-sky, a Russian-born Jewish writer and playwright who is known mainly as the author of *The Dybbuk* (original title, *Between Two Worlds*).[15] In 1908, he moved to St. Petersburg, joined the Jewish Historic-Ethnographic Society, and in a ground-breaking article, "Jewish Folk Creation," he presented Jewish folklore as of equal value to the folklore of the European nations. From then until his death in 1920, An-sky devoted his life to systematic, comprehensive ethnographic research of East European Jewry. The high point of his activity was the organization of an ethnographic expedition for collecting Jewish folk literary works. The expedition operated in 1912–1914 and covered some 70 Jewish villages and towns in Ukraine, documenting thousands of folktales, songs, ceremonies, customs, sayings, blessings and so on. In addition, hundreds of documents, letters, manuscripts, community registers, as well as some seven hundred items of religious, historic, or artistic value were collected. On the basis of this collection, in 1917 An-sky founded the Central Jewish Museum in St. Petersburg. The museum functioned intermittently until 1929, when it was closed by order of the Soviet government. Today, part of its collections are held by the Ethnographic Museum in St. Petersburg (Lokin, 1994).

3.c. First Steps in Palestine Ethnography

Both the museums established in Palestine and the Jewish museums founded in Europe ignored the ethnography of the inhabitants of Palestine. The Christian religious background of the founders of the Palestine museums resulted in most of them focusing on archeology, and they generally stressed findings from biblical times and the Second Temple period. The museums of the European research societies also exhibited collections from the field of natural sciences, which were considered of interest mainly in conjunction with the study of the

Holy Scriptures. The church museums, in contrast, tended to exhibit ritual objects, priestly garb, and ancient manuscripts kept in their libraries. The Jewish museums in Europe, even though they were ethnographic, did not deal at all with Judaism in Palestine. So, in spite of the blossoming of scientific research and the establishment of many museums toward the close of the nineteenth century (Shai, 2006, 230–31,)[16] ethnographic research focusing on the daily life of the inhabitants of Palestine was quite limited and uninspiring.

The first person to take an interest in collecting ethnographic objects in Palestine was almost certainly the American consul Selah Merrill, who served as consul in Jerusalem from time-to-time, for 16 years between 1882 and 1906, and spent further time in the region as a member of various scientific expeditions. Merrill amassed impressive collections in the various scientific fields, including the ethnography of the inhabitants of Palestine, Arabs and Jews. Most of them he sold to universities in the United States. For example, the list of finds he turned over to the possession of Harvard University included, among other things, "weapons used by the Bedouins; decorative appurtenances for horses; *tefillin* and a *shofar*; writing implements; clothing, shoes, and jewelry worn in Palestine; jars, pails, and leather water skins; weights; books; musical instruments; many objects illustrating the life of the urban, rural, and Bedouin inhabitants" (Kark, 2000).

The first museum in Palestine that regularly offered exhibits of Jewish ethnography was the Bezalel Museum, which is considered by many the "real" first museum in Palestine.[17] The museum was founded in 1906 by the artist and art scholar Boris Schatz as part of the Bezalel Academy of Arts and Crafts and as part of the efforts by members of the New Yishuv in Jerusalem to establish national educational and cultural institutions such as libraries, institutions of higher education and the like (Ben-Arieh, 1979, 573–96). Bezalel was defined as a general national museum and in its early years focused on three main topics: archeology, nature, and art. Included in the field of art, among other things, was Judaica and Jewish folk art (Kol-Inbar, 1992). The latter, however, received place of pride fairly late; see below.

3.d The British Mandate Period

The First World War and the British Mandate that followed it led to wide-ranging developments in the Palestine region, which did not bypass the museums in it. In Jerusalem, more museums were founded by western research societies, whose work yielded findings unprecedented in scope. In the early twentieth century, a number of large, modern museums opened in the city, some of which still operate today: in 1921, the British Mandate authorities founded the Rockefeller Archeological Museum (in time, the Rockefeller Museum) (Sussman and Reich, 1987), and in 1922 the Muslim Waqf established the Islamic Museum on the Temple Mount (Salameh, 2001). As time went on, members of the New Hebrew Yishuv founded the first museums outside of Jerusalem: the Tel Aviv Museum of Art (1932); the Museum of Art (1938) and Bet Shturman (1941) in Ein Hod; Gordon House in Deganiah Aleph (1941); and other small museums, all out of deep commitment to the values of the Zionist movement (Kol-Inbar, 1992).

The ethnographic museums, too, underwent a surge of significant development during the Mandate. In 1920, the archeology and nature collections of Bezalel were transferred to new museums focused exclusively on these fields. Bezalel remained a museum for general and Jewish art, including Judaica, numismatics, and Jewish ethnography. As part of the plan for changes, Boris Schatz suggested establishing an ethnography hall, in which mannequins representing the various Jewish types would be set against a backdrop of holy sites in Palestine. Even though this plan never came to fruition, the ethnographic collection expanded and included items from the field of folk art, ritual objects, *ketubbot* (marriage contracts), accessories for Jewish holidays, and so on. In time, under the directorship of Mordechai Narkiss, the museum added temporary exhibitions alongside the permanent displays; some focused on a topic of Jewish ethnography. For instance, in 1940, an exhibit was produced devoted to Yemenite Jewry—apparently the first such in Palestine, and perhaps in the entire world, dedicated to non-European Jewry (Kol-Inbar, 1992).

Like Jewish folklore, Arab popular culture also garnered scant attention at the beginning of the twentieth century from scholars of culture. Both intellectual Arabs, as well as Western scholars, preferred to deal with the classic written culture (Sowayan, 1993). This is true many times over regarding Palestinian culture, which prior to 1948 was not considered independent. The first ethnographic exhibit devoted to the Arabs living in Palestine was mounted in 1922 in the Old City Citadel. Turning the Citadel into a new municipal museum occurred under the aegis of the Pro-Jerusalem Society and at the initiative of Charles Robert Ashbee.[18] Ashbee was a well-known British architect who had been invited to advise on the planning of Jerusalem by Robert Storrs, the British Military Governor of Jerusalem. Among his many activities, Ashbee was one of the main members of the British Arts & Crafts movement, which dealt with the preservation and dissemination of utile arts and crafts. Owing to that, the ethnographic exhibit that he curated in Jerusalem focused on crafts and local industry. Ashbee himself collected all the housewares displayed in the exhibit on trips he made for that purpose in the Arab villages and large cities throughout Israel (Ben-Arieh, 2001; Heisler-Rubin, 2005, 96; *Exhibition of Palestine* 1922).

The first museum in Palestine devoted entirely to Arab Palestinian ethnography was the Palestine Folk Museum, established in 1935 at the initiative of the British high commissioner Arthur Wauchope. It was founded with the intent of preserving the local material culture of Arab inhabitants of Israel—fellahin and Bedouins—which had begun to disappear owing to accelerated processes of modernization. The collection contained 1,600 items: mainly local costumes, as well as housewares, religious and ritual appurtenances, weapons, musical instruments, and agricultural implements. After a few years in which it was not allotted a permanent home, it was finally housed in the Citadel and operated there until the 1948 war (Cohen-Hattab, 2006, 146–48; Bar-Adon, 1941).

3.e *The State of Israel in Its Early Years*

If the change of rule in 1917 led to momentum in the development of museums in Mandate Palestine, the establishment of the State of Israel resulted in an actual revolution. In the formative years of the state, its various institutions dealt with vigorous educational activity whose aim was the formation of ideological cohesiveness among "the Jewish people," "the Jewish nation," and "Eretz Israel," and firmly rooting its "natural and historical" right to the land.[19] One of the ways in which this aim was achieved was the establishment of museums. They were presented as a Zionist project of the "young state," which was intended to reveal and introduce its past as "an ancient nation with a diverse population" (Rahmani, 1976, 7–8). Toward that aim several archeological museums were founded, which presented findings from the distant Jewish past of Israel while at the same time blurring its recent—Arab—past.[20] In the 1950s and the early 1960s, dozens of such museums were founded throughout Israel. Most of them were located in agricultural settlements, especially kibbutzim, in which the working of the land yielded many archeological findings (Inbar, 1988, 10).

In the early years of the State of Israel, the field of ethnography was characterized mainly by attempts to save the remnants of the material culture of European Jewry. Government institutions, public associations, and private collectors tried to lay their hands on as many items as possible that could attest to the rich cultural life destroyed in the Holocaust. This endeavor, however, was secondary and took place in the shadow of the main effort to document and expose the horrors of the Holocaust itself. Of course, the Yad Vashem Museum, as well as others devoted to the Holocaust, displayed objects that were in daily use by the Jews of Europe, but these are shown not for their cultural value, but rather as symbolic of the community that had been obliterated.

In addition, in those years of "mass immigration," entire Jewish communities immigrated to Israel from around the world, and with their arrival, accelerated processes began of assimilation into the new society and abandonment of their previous culture. Even though, as stated, the emphasis in those years was on rescuing remnants of European Jewry, a number of elements were involved in an attempt to document and preserve the culture of the new immigrant communities. This activity was led by the Bezalel Museum in Jerusalem, the Eretz Israel Museum in Tel Aviv, the Ethnographic and Folklore Museum in Haifa, and later, the Israel Museum, which inherited the Bezalel collections.

In the 1960s and 1970s, public interest in archeology declined and with it the establishment of archeological museums slowed down. In this period, a great increase occurred in the museums on the history of Jewish settlement. The largest of them present a panoramic review of the history of Zionist settlement in Palestine, starting from the 1880s through to the establishment of the State of Israel, while the smaller ones are usually dedicated to the local history of a single settlement or a limited area. Within a few years, dozens of such museums were founded in veteran settlement sites all over Israel, including kibbutzim, moshavim, and even moshavot that in the meantime had turned into cities. The museum was located, in most instances, in early buildings of the settlements, which were restored and preserved for this purpose. In the 1980s, 30 such museums were established and by the end of the 1990s they made up one-third of all museums in Israel (Stein, 1998, 102–6).

3.f. The Growth of Single-Ethnic Museums in Israel

The beginning of the ethnographic museums devoted to a single ethnic group should be examined against the background of the far-reaching changes that occurred in public discourse in Israel in the 1960s and 1970s, among them the increased inter-ethnic tension between Ashkenazic and non-Ashkenazic Jews ("Mizrahim"). Sami Shalom Chetrit defines the 1960s, from the Wadi Salib riots (1959) to the founding of the Black Panthers (1971), as the period that led "from the cultural 'melting pot' to the social 'pressure cooker'" (Chetrit, 2004, 102). The Black Panthers brought into public awareness the distress of the Mizrahim in Israel in all its direness and their being relegated to the geographic, economic, and political margins of the State of Israel. The 1977 elections, which resulted in the end of a 30-year rule of Mapai, are considered the high point in the Mizrahi struggle (Ibid., 314). In this period the myth of national unity was torn asunder and the ethnic fissures existing in Israeli society were exposed in their entirety. The idea of the "intermingling of the Diasporas" and "the melting pot," which strove to create a homogenous society, was replaced by recognition of the many cultures existing within Israeli culture, with its tensions and its complexity (Eisenstadt, 2002, 264). While trying to shake off and rebel against the establishment's attempt to erase their cultures, different groups in Israeli society began precisely to stress it, to emphasize its uniqueness and distinctiveness in contrast to the dominant Ashkenazic culture (Yonah, 2005, 13).

During the tenure of the Eighth Knesset (1973–1977—the Knesset that preceded the political turnabout), a number of Knesset members (MKs) of Iraqi, Yemenite, and Moroccan origin led a penetrating discussion about inter-ethnic group tension. As part of their activity, in 1974, the first discussion dealing with the heritage of Mizrahi Jewry was held in the Knesset (Jablonka, 2008), 154–56). In 1976, the Knesset Education and Culture Committee convened a one-day seminar on "The Heritage of Eastern Jewry," with the participation of MKs, historians, and educators, which extensively discussed the education system's ignoring the history and heritage of Mizrahi Jewry (Bar-Asher, 1976). These discussions roused the government to action, and at the end of the 1970s, the Education Ministry established "The Center for the Integration of the Heritage of Sephardic and Mizrahi Jews," with the aim of developing content related to the history and heritage of Eastern Jewry and of implementing it within the curricula (Cohen, 2002, 5–8; Bar-Levav, 2002). As a result of these and other activities, a crack opened in the uniform narrative studied in the education system and an opportunity was created for a more pluralistic study of history (Ben-Amos, 1995; Naveh and Yogev, 2002).

This is the platform on which there began to arise, at an ever-increasing pace, associations and societies for the nurturing of the heritage and culture of specific ethnic groups, and along with them the first ethnic group museums. As early as the end of the 1970s there coalesced the nucleus of the museum for Yemenite Jewish heritage of the Association for the Fostering of Society and Culture in Netanya, the Museum for the History of German Jewry in Nahariya, and the Museum of Italian Jewry in Jerusalem. In 1977, the Babylonian Jewry Heritage Museum was inaugurated in Or Yehuda; it was the first institution of its type, whose establishment was preceded by political activity and by wide-ranging fundraising. These enabled, for the first time, the erection of a building in which activity was concentrated. This center, which also conducts—in addition to the museum—research activity, a publication arm, and political and social conferences, has constituted since its founding a model for imitation for other communities.

Other ethnic museums arose in the 1980s and since then their rate of establishment has continuously increased. As Yehudit Inbar wrote in a guide to museums published in 1990:

> Recently, many museums have formed around the issue of ethnic groups. One may consider them historical museums and not ethnographic ones, even though items and objects belonging to everyday life and folklore are displayed in them. In distinction from the accepted ethnographic displays, in which objects of material culture are exhibited through a distanced, aesthetic approach, in these places they serve to illustrate the history of the group and its culture … these museums are a chapter in the integration of the ethnic groups into Israel, and they are created out of concern for preservation of tradition and heritage for future generations (Inbar and Schiller, 1990, 23).

Following the Jewish communities, non-Jewish ones as well began to establish museums and heritage centers dealing with their culture. In the 1980s and 1990s, a number of Bedouin, Druze, and Circassian museums were founded. In the same vein, Palestinian museums developed, some have been in existences for decades, and they are a direct continuation of the first ethnographic museums established in pre-Mandate Palestine, described at the beginning of this chapter.

Chapter 4

❦

"National" Museums

The idea of establishing a museum in Israel that would tell the story of the Jewish people was raised, as noted, as early as the end of the nineteenth century, and was realized partially with the establishment of the Bezalel Museum in Jerusalem in the early twentieth century, as described above. In the early 1950s, after the establishment of the State of Israel, other, small ethnographic museums were created in Tel Aviv and Haifa for this purpose. The founding event, however, of ethnographic museums in Israel was undoubtedly the opening of the Israel Museum in Jerusalem, which has an ethnography wing. Under its auspices—for the first time—orderly, systematic ethnographic research was conducted on the various ethnic communities. As time went on, other museums were established devoted to the story of the Jewish people throughout time. The most striking of them is the Museum of the Jewish People (Beit Hatfutsot) in Tel Aviv and the Wolfson Museum for Jewish Art in Jerusalem.

In distinction from museums dedicated to one group, the museums designated here as "national" claim to present a comprehensive picture of the Jewish people with all its variety of ethnic groups. In this chapter, I will describe these museums, the first of which served as the foundation out of which later grew dozens of ethnic museums.

4.a. The Israel Museum–Jerusalem

The idea of founding the Israel Museum arose in the early 1950s. The director of the Bezalel Museum, Mordecai Narkiss, hoped to significantly expand that museum and conceived a plan to erect a new, larger structure. At the same time, the government Department of Antiquities needed a new, central museum for archeology resulting from the loss of access to the Rockefeller Museum, which after the 1948 war remained in East Jerusalem under Jordanian control. In the early 1960s, substantial impetus for establishing the museum occurred at the initiative of Teddy Kollek, who acted to promote the issue when he served as the director of the Prime Minister's Office under David Ben-Gurion. In 1964, Kollek left that position and devoted himself entirely to leading the campaign to see the museum become a reality. The Israel Museum was opened on 11 May 1965 and Kollek was its first director. He continued to raise money and contributions of items for the museum even after he was elected mayor of Jerusalem (Tamir, 1990, 7).

Despite the museum's name and its location in Givat Ram, close to the Israeli government institutions, the Israel Museum is not defined as a national museum, and it is not an official state museum founded on behalf of the State of Israel and with its funding.[21] Martin Weyl, the general director of the museum from 1981 to 1996, relates that the museum directorate insisted that it not be defined by law as a national museum, so that it would enjoy professional administration and artistic freedom and not be subject to political pressure on the part of those he called "our neighbors across the road," that is, the Knesset and government ministries (Kollek et al., 1990, 49). Despite this, the founders of the museum undoubtedly designated a national role for the museum in unifying the nation and consolidating its historical narrative. In one of its first publications, the museum was presented as follows: "It represents the overall Jewish experience and constitutes a cross-section of four thousand years of Hebrew history, a spectrum of a people that survived many travails with great tenacity over a long period of time and over greater geographical distances than any other nation" (Katz, 1968, 31).

Against that backdrop, the Israel Museum was the object of criticism from different directions. From the right side of the political spectrum, art critic Miriam Tal published a review of the museum about a year after it opened. Tal wrote that it is not a faithful follower of the path of the Bezalel Museum, since it does not have a separate department for Hebrew art, but displays the works of Jewish artists together with general art. She claims that thereby it falters in the "national-educational task imposed on it from the outset" (Tal, 1966, 561).[22] Similarly, three decades later, advertising executive Eitan Dor-Shav argued that the Israel Museum's topical structure contributes to "a loss of national memory," in that it removes the displayed items from their "natural" context and does not create an orderly narrative of the history of the Jewish people (Dor-Shav, 1998, 104).

Conversely, the anthropologist Kaylin Goldstein argues that the Israel Museum has always taken an active role in institutionalizing the Ashkenazic-Jewish elite and in Orientalistic patronizing of Mizrahi and Arab culture (Goldstein, 2005, 27–29). In a similar vein, the psychoanalyst and curator Itamar Levi wrote that the archeology branch of the museum does not relate at all to the Arab history of the region, but rather "presents a political, consensual, official narrative" as part of its "educational-propagandistic" function (Levi, 1996, 4). In response to Levi's comment, the then-general director of the museum, Martin Weyl, repeated the statement that contrary to the prevailing notion the institution is not a national museum. Moreover, Weyl argued that the "Israel Museum does not try to tell a story; it is not a historical museum" (Weyl, 1996, 4). Even now, tension reigns between those striving to stress the universal nature of the museum and those interested in seeing it as a state-national institution (Rapp, 2005).

From the time of its founding the Israel Museum included an ethnography department, whose head was the curator Aviva Muller-Lancet, a disciple of the folklore professor Dov Noy.[23] The department was established out of a sense of urgency, with the aim of rescuing as much as possible of the cultural treasures of the Jews who had come to Israel during the time of the mass immigration, part of whom had already been assimilated into Israeli society and had abandoned their ancient customs. At first, the department was based solely on the large collection that had come from the Bezalel Museum, which for the most part had never been displayed for lack of space. The high point of this legacy was a rare, priceless collection of items that had been acquired from Yemenite Jewish communities while still living in Yemen, in the 1920s and 1930s. In 1940, a temporary exhibit was held in Bezalel that was based on this collection, but, after that, it was forgotten and ignored. When the collection was transferred to its new home in the Israel Museum, it turned out that the documentary information that had accompanied the exhibits had been lost. Department workers devoted one of their first projects to research among Yemenite Jews in Israel in an attempt to reconstruct the misplaced data about the various items in the collection. In addition to the Yemenite Jewry collection, the ethnography department had a collection with 1,400 items that had been acquired from North African Jewish—mainly Moroccan—communities, both urban and rural ones—some in remote regions in the Atlas Mountains (Department of Ethnography 1971).

Understanding that a museum the size of the Israel Museum cannot suffice with representing only two Jewish communities (Yemen and Morocco), Muller-Lancet devoted effort to establishing a new collection that would focus on Bukharan Jewry. To that end, she conducted comprehensive ethnographic research, made connections with a number of senior community members, and acquired from Bukharan Jews who were already living in Israel item-after-item (Muller-Lancet, 1974, 3–4). The result was presented in 1967–1968, in an exhibition devoted to Bukharan Jewry—the first temporary exhibition of the Ethnography Department (Muller-Lancet, 1968). The space allotted to the exhibition was relatively small, and most of the objects displayed were clothing items and jewelry. The nature of the exhibition and the criteria by which decisions were made as to which items would be included were only esthetic, and no information was provided to the visitors as to the original context of use for the objects shown. The department staff felt that the many visitors were satisfied by the exhibition, especially those coming from rural areas, for whom this was their first visit to the museum. Many perceived the exhibit as a source of pride, since objects generally considered worthless were displayed as equal to world famous art works. The very mounting of the exhibition even led to the contribution of additional objects from among the families who visited it (Department of Ethnography 1971).

The Bukhara exhibition was the first in a tradition of temporary exhibits by the Ethnography Department, each of which featured one Jewish community. In every instance, the department staff conducted in-depth research about a single group and presented the findings in an exhibition. These, in turn, enabled the development of the department's permanent exhibition, described below. In 1973, the second large exhibition was held—on Moroccan Jewry. It was included in the celebrations of the twenty-fifth anniversary of the State of Israel and owing to that was awarded a relatively large budget and received a great deal of publicity. To endow it with a "national" nature, political pressure was applied to the curators to change the character of the exhibition so that it would include other North African communities, or even all the Jewish communities that had lived in Muslim countries. The museum refused by arguing that it would be preferable to mount an in-depth exhibition focusing on one group rather than have a superficial display encompassing many communities (Muller-Lancet, 1974).

In contrast to the planning of the exhibit on Bukharan Jewry, which as noted was guided solely by esthetic considerations, for the exhibit on Moroccan Jewry educational aims were defined in advance, with an eye on two types of audiences. On the one hand, the exhibition was intended for people originating from Morocco, their descendants and other Jews who had emigrated from Islamic countries, with the aim of renewing their sense of pride in their culture, a feeling that had been harmed in the heavy-handed "melting pot" policy in Israel. On the other hand, the intention was that the exhibition would also attract Israelis who come from European countries and change the somewhat prejudicial view they had about Moroccan and Mizrahi Jews. Muller-Lancet turned to many Moroccan immigrants in an attempt to involve them in preparation of the exhibition. Some responded happily and with great willingness to contribute knowledge and objects. Others, many from among the more educated members of the community, expressed their concern that this would be a folklore exhibit that would present them in a distorted way as a "primitive tribe" (Muller-Lancet, 1974, 3–4).

As a result of these fears, it was deliberately decided that the nature of the exhibition would not be scientific—"objective,"—but rather that it would be slanted toward the positive and present an ideal picture of the life of the Jewish community in Morocco. The clothing items and jewelry in the original Bezalel collection were not sufficient for that aim, since they were based on relatively poor rural communities. In an attempt to switch the emphasis of the exhibition to the urban communities with a more modern way of life, Muller-Lancet sought to obtain new items from well-situated members of the urban communities. Beyond that, Muller-Lancet collected objects illustrating the spiritual contribution of the Moroccan Jewish community to overall Jewish culture. Likewise, chosen for the image collection accompanying the exhibition were only photos that showed Moroccan Jews in a positive light, while rejected for presentation were pictures showing people in a poor environment, with torn or worn clothing, or with an unhappy or undignified visage (Muller-Lancet, 1974, 5–6).

When the exhibition was on display, the museum staff kept a written record of the visitors' reactions. Muller-Lancet summarizes that many visitors were excited by the appearance of certain objects, mainly those taken from daily life, such as clothing items or a baby's cradle. Ritual objects and historical items garnered less attention. At the same time, a significant number of visitors with a Moroccan background expressed doubt about the ability of Ashkenazic Israelis to understand their culture. Indeed, Muller-Lancet notes that Ashkenazic visitors reported that they enjoyed the exhibition but did not comprehend what they saw. Despite all the foregoing, the show was considered a success and was able to draw many new visitors to the museum who would not have come otherwise (Muller-Lancet, 1974, 14–15).[24]

The next target selected for a temporary exhibit was Kurdish Jewry. While for the topics of Bukharan and Morocco Jewry, the museum had available the old Bezalel collections, for the Jews of Kurdistan there was no such assemblage, and the preparatory work had to start from scratch. The budget allotted for the research and for acquiring objects was low and insufficient; apparently because this topic was of low priority for the museum directors. Owing to the success of the exhibit on Moroccan Jewry, Muller-Lancet was able to convince the Education Ministry that there was an urgent need for systematic ethnographic field research among the various immigrant communities that had come to Israel (Muller-Lancet, 1993, 292, 287–302; Domínguez, 1989, 111–12).

The research began in 1974 and was conducted for some seven years, during which the curator Ora Schwartz-Be'eri visited hundreds of homes of Israelis of Kurdish origin, and even went for a tour of Iran. In light of the lack of cooperation on the part of the population in selling objects for the exhibit, Muller-Lancet wrote an article for the periodical of Kurdish Jews, in which she told about the work being carried out by the museum and about its importance for the Kurdish Jewish community (Muller-Lancet 1978). Ultimately, the new collection amassed over 300 objects and the exhibit was displayed in 1981–1982 (Schwartz-Be'eri, 1982, 13). From then until now the Ethnography Department has mounted other exhibits about the Jewish communities of Spain (1989), the Alsace region (1991), India (1995), Afghanistan (1997), Yemen (2000), and the Caucasus (2001) (Juhasz, 1989; Muchawsky-Schnapper, 1991; Slapak, 1995; Ben-Yosef, 1997; Muchawsky-Schnapper, 2000; Mikdash-Shamailov, 2001).

All of these were shown in the Ethnography Department, which until recently was physically and structurally separated from the Jewish Art (Judaica) Department. This artificial division on many an occasion raised questions when new items came into the possession of the museum as to which department was responsible for them. The key to the division was such that most often the Judaica Department received the items that contained any kind of inscription, such as Torah scrolls, ritual objects and the like. Clothing, jewelry, and housewares that did not contain any inscription went to the Ethnography Department.[25] A situation was created such that certain collections were split between two departments in an almost arbitrary manner. For example, from the circumcision ritual, the *mohel's* (ritual circumciser) tools would go to the Judaica Department, while the traditional infant clothing went to the Ethnography Department.[26] Moreover, the fact that the Ethnography Department did not contain objects with Jewish inscriptions led to rather complex struggles to define the artifacts as "Jewish" objects. The workers in the department had constant recourse to the question of whether the costumes and objects presented have a "Jewish character," or are they ultimately identical to those used by the non-Jews in the same places (Fenichel, 2005, 92). For these reasons, and with the aim of presenting the different communities in a more complete way, the two departments were finally merged into one called the "Department for Jewish Art and Ethnography" (Rapp, 2005, 66). Yet this change was only organizational, yielding no change in the display.[27] Between 2007 and 2010, comprehensive renovations were carried out in the permanent exhibit of the entire museum, and the department changed its name to the "Department for Jewish Art and Life." This time, extensive changes were made to the exhibition, but still not conceptual ones.

The new exhibition is divided into five topical sections. In the center of the display is the "Synagogue Route," which contains four synagogues brought to the museum in their entirety with all their content: from the cities Horb, Germany; Cochin, India; Vittorio Veneto, Italy; and Paramaribo, Suriname.[28] The exhibition space called "Illuminating the Script" offers a selection of rare illustrated Hebrew manuscripts from the Middle Ages and the Renaissance, including the Torah, Haggadot, and other parts of the Holy Scriptures. The three rooms of "The Cycle of the Jewish Year" present items and ritual objects related to festivals and other occasions by topic: "The Sabbath and the Pilgrimage Holidays," "Holidays and Days of Remembrance," and "Miracle Festivals."

Ethnographically, the most interesting two spaces of the exhibition are those located at the two ends of the wing, in which far-reaching changes were made in the new display. The first, "The Rhythm of Life," contains objects related to birth, marriage, and death. In the previous exhibition, as it was before 2007, life cycle rites were presented, with each one illustrated by one community, and the accompanying explanation relating the essence of the rite and the main differences in the way it was conducted by different groups—most often a comparison between Ashkenazic communities and Sephardic and Mizrahi ones. For example, the different marriage ceremonies are presented separately: the henna ceremony as held in Morocco, an engagement ceremony as it was in Afghanistan, the *huppah* (wedding canopy) as it appeared in Turkey, the *yihud* (seclusion) of the couple as was done in Kurdistan, and finally a modern room in which "an assimilated [German couple] … who were married by the Rabbinate or perhaps in the municipality." In the new exhibition, there is no specific place for each group, and more emphasis is placed on the objects themselves.

The final exhibition section, "Costume and Jewelry: A Matter of Identity," is devoted, according to the explanatory sign at the entrance to "a comparative impression and examination of every-day life in the different communities … and of reciprocity between the communities and their non-Jewish surroundings." Also noted is that "as a result of serious political and economic turmoil, not many household objects or items of clothing were preserved that would have been worthwhile including in this exhibition. Owing to that, not all communities are represented to a degree befitting their culture and tradition; this applies especially to East European communities." Thus, the exhibition contains mainly holiday garb of the Mizrahi communities, such as bridal dresses from Yemen, Cochin, and Afghanistan. Also present are a few every-day clothing items of both Mizrahi Jewish communities as well as East European ones. The former permanent exhibition included a selection of *talitot* (prayer shawls) as well as a display devoted to various clothing orders and regulations imposed upon Jews in all periods and all communities, from the eighth-century Muslim regulations to the Nazi German laws in the twentieth century. These two elements are missing in the new exhibition.

FIGURE 1 | *Candle Lighting, Israel Museum, Jerusalem, April 2007*

It is clear that the wing is arranged in an attempt to stress the characteristics that are similar among the different communities and to present them as members of a single nation linked by the Jewish religion. The way in which the exhibits are arranged does, of course, allow for comparison between the various groups and even the accompanying explanations tell of the differences in their customs. At the same time, the very organization of the exhibit as a topical cross-section stresses the component of religion (the Sabbath, religious works, ritual objects, holiday appurtenances, synagogues, marriage) as part of the emphasis on ethnic identity. The cultural heritage of each community is broken down into elements and placed as a kind of piece in the puzzle of the Jewish people, in a way that does not enable the visitors to gain a separate impression of each community in its own right.

In addition, the uniformity of the temporary exhibits mounted over the years have sometimes revealed insensitivity. A case in point, the exhibition on Yemenite Jewry (2000) focused almost exclusively on the community around San'a and consciously ignored other communities throughout Yemen that differed in their customs and garb. Yet, this decision was not brought to the attention of those visiting the exhibit, which was presented as comprising all of Yemenite Jewry (Muchawsky-Schnapper, 2000, 8). In the exhibition on the Jews of India (1995), the opposite phenomenon occurred. The Indian Jews were divided into three separate communities: Bnei Israel, Cochin, and Baghdadi. Each community has its own history, and each was located in a completely different geographical region, so that they barely had contact with each other. Yet, they were presented in a joint exhibition, "only because they all stemmed from the large subcontinent of India" (Slepak, 1995, 8). This is, of course, a legitimate decision, but it attests to a certain order of priorities that prevented focusing and going into depth about each one of the three communities. This was startling, especially in light of the exhibition that preceded it, which concentrated on the Jewry of the Alsace region in France, without adding other European communities to it (Muchawsky-Schnapper, 1991).

Oriental paternalism also occurs in the way the department is divided into Judaica and Ethnography. The Judaica Department places emphasis on European Jewry, while the Ethnography Department represents mainly the Mizrahi *edot*. The temporary exhibitions held over the years in the Ethnography Wing, as described above, were devoted in the main to Mizrahi groups. In 1990, Teddy Kollek, referring to the activity of the Ethnography Department, said that it has tremendous, ongoing influence in the realm of preserving the neglected heritage of Mizrahi Jewry so that the entire museum thereby contributes "something to building the nation" (Kollek et al., 1990, 43). The mainstays of the museum boasted of the sense of pride and belonging that the exhibition nurtured among the Jewish visitors of Mizrahi origin and did not hide their hope that it would help them "become better citizens" (Katz, 1968, 30).

In summation, the Jewish Art and Life Wing relates the story of the Jewish people from the point of view of the Zionist movement, which sees it as a unified body whose common features prevail over differences and whose place is in the Land of Israel. The display that best illustrates the way in which the Wing fosters Zionist values is the *tallit* discovered at Masada. Instead of offering it in the Archeology Wing, the museum professionals chose to show it here, in the center of the display of the "Diaspora" *talitot* from recent centuries. The Masada myth is well-rooted in collective Zionist consciousness and "recruiting" it for this wing of the museum presents the Jews of the Diaspora, as people returning home and stresses their right to the Land of Israel.[29]

4.b. Eretz Israel Museum—Tel Aviv

After the establishment of Israel, the antiquities collector Dr. Walter Moses offered to donate his collections to the Tel Aviv municipality, on the condition that it would create a museum to contain them. Moses' collections were organized according to the raw material from which the exhibits were made. His vision was that each collection would have its own pavilion, which in effect, would operate as an independent museum: the glass pavilion, the copper pavilion, the ceramics pavilion, and so on. The site chosen for the complex of museums was a hill in the Ramat Aviv neighborhood, which had been until 1948 the site of the Palestinian village of Sheikh Munis and in which only a few years earlier an archeological excavation had been carried out on the remains of a Philistine city, namely, Tel Qasile. The museum complex was inaugurated in 1953 as the Haaretz Museum. Over the years the museum's collections mushroomed, and other museums throughout Tel Aviv became part of it: Independence Hall, the Museum of the History of Tel Aviv–Yafo, and others (Ze'evi, 1983/4, 247).

One of the pavilions is devoted to ethnography and folklore, but it came into being only after the museum's opening, since the Moses collections did not include items from the field of folk art. The pavilion's beginnings stem from 1950, when the Circle for Jewish Folk Art "Ginza" was founded in Tel Aviv, with the aim of rescuing and preserving the remains of Jewish art from Eastern Europe. The Circle's collection and library were located in a building on Bialik Street in Tel Aviv.[30] In the 1950s and early 1960s, the Circle held a variety of exhibitions in the Tel Aviv Museum of Art, which were devoted to topics such as Hanukkah lamps, *hadassim* (Havdalah spice boxes), *ketubbot* (marriage contracts), paper cuttings, woodcrafts, and synagogues in Spain ("'Ginza' Circle and Its Activities" 1961, 18–19). In 1961, the Ginza collection was put at the disposal of Haaretz Museum under the directorship of David Davidovitch, a scholar of European folk culture, who specialized in the study of synagogues in Poland ("Ginza—Museum for Jewish Folk Art 1962, 17). Selected to house the collection was the home of the Baydas family, which was one of the few structures still remaining from the village of Sheikh Munis. The building was emptied of its tenants and added to the area of Haaretz Museum. In 1963, the pavilion with the name of "The Ethnography and Folklore Pavilion" was officially inaugurated. The Ginza collection was exhibited on the lower floor in the "Section for Religious Art." On the other two floors the "*Edot* Section" was established, which was based mainly on the clothing of the communities and nations that had been collected by the "Association for National Garb." Among other things, displayed in it were marriage ceremonies of Yemenite and Bukharan Jewry, Sabbath eve in a Polish Jewish home, and mannequins representing life in an Eastern European shtetl ([Davidovitch], 1963, 19; [Davidovitch], 1968, 61–62; Bachi, 1987, 183–84).

In the 1980s the Haaretz Museum's directorate, headed by Rehavam Ze'evi, realized that the museum was not achieving its educational goal, since it was dealing with too many topics ("almost every subject except for art") among which there was practically no common denominator. Since every topic was displayed in a separate pavilion, the museum actually constituted an "assemblage of different museums with no intellectual or topical link among them" (Ze'evi, 1983/4, 247–49). To improve the situation, for the first time a master plan was prepared for the museum that stressed the intellectual and content aspects. It was decided that the main topic the museum would deal with would be "Eretz Israel," among other reasons, as an antithesis to the Diaspora-stressing Beit Hatfutsot. As a consequence, the museum's name was changed from "Haaretz Museum" to "Eretz Israel Museum—Tel Aviv." Ze'evi explained;

> When Beit Hatfutsot was inaugurated five years ago and succeeded in bringing information about the Diaspora, the Dispersal, and the Holocaust to the awareness of its

visitors, the need for a parallel, complementary museum became even more striking, one that would cover the topic of Eretz Israel. The Beit Hatfutsot visitor sees the glory of the cultural output of the Jewish people in the Diaspora and asks: "And the continuation?" The visitor there sees the Exile that is petering out and asks about the solution. The Jewish people, which succeeded in building Beit Hatfutsot, was obligated to erect the Eretz Israel Museum at the same time (Ze'evi, 1983/4, 49).

As part of the plan, new pavilions were to be created, including the "Pavilion of Jewish Communities," which was to replace the old Ethnography and Folklore Pavilion. The intention was to expand its display significantly so that "the role of each *edah* in the building of Israel would be presented." In addition, there was supposed to be a "Minorities Pavilion," which would offer the culture of the Arabs, the Christians, the Druze, and the Circassians living in Israel (Ze'evi, 1983/4, 259). These plans were never realized and the pavilion remained unchanged. Of note is that since the museum opened, the Ethnography Pavilion has been situated at the edge, in a location distant from the entrance and center of the museum. It is isolated from the other pavilions. Had the new pavilions been erected, it would have created a structural continuum that would have linked the Ethnography and Folklore Pavilion to the center of the museum's area and made it more accessible to the visitors.[31]

The Ethnography and Folklore Pavilion was closed in 1981 following a robbery and reopened about a year later (in 1983, some of the stolen objects were found). On Purim 1982, an event was held in the pavilion centering on clothing of *edot,* at which there also appeared folklore troupes, and a competition of ethnic costumes took place

("Review of the Museum's Activities in 1976–1983" 1983/84, 276–77). Since then the pavilion's exhibit has hardly changed. The main hall is devoted to Jewish holidays and presents them in calendrical order, displaying the related artifacts (Hanukkah lamps, dreidls, etc.), along with explanations about each holiday and its meaning.[32] The side room offers ketubbot from different places. Another corner features the Sabbath and its customs.

FIGURE 2 | *The Sabbath in Custom and Object,*
Eretz Israel Museum, Tel Aviv, July 2008

On both sides are two rooms, each of which presents two *edot:* Moroccan Jewry, Bukharan Jewry; Yemenite Jewry, and Kurdish Jewry. Each group is featured in a different corner displaying clothing, jewelry, and various housewares ("an urban living room" is displayed in the Moroccan Jewry corner). The only significant addition to the pavilion since the early 1980s, is the exhibit of the Trino Vercellese synagogue brought from Italy in its entirety in 1973. The synagogue was displayed for a few years after its arrival, but the current exhibit opened in 2003 (Davidovitch, 1976, 215–17).

In 2013, the museum mounted an exhibition about Ethiopian Jewry. For the first time in Israel, the Ethiopian Jewish community was shown in its complete historical-cultural-social context and not only through the lens of immigration to Israel and the problems involved. So, for example, the exhibit gave pivotal space to the founding myths of Ethiopian nationality as well, not necessarily from a Jewish point of view (Yardai, 2013). The exhibition's curator did not even shy away from the discrimination and prejudice the Ethiopian Jewish emigres encounter in Israel. In the exhibit's catalog, she expressed hope that becoming familiar with the rich, complex history of the Ethiopian Jews would help Israeli society "flourish in cultural diversity, to be built up from the common denominator and to reinforce itself also on the basis of the difference" (Turel, 2013). If this trend should continue, then similar to what is being done in the Israel Museum, the permanent exhibit of the Ethnography Pavilion will continue to stress the common denominator of the Jewish people, while the self-identity of each community will be presented through temporary exhibitions.

4.c. Museum for Ethnology and Folklore—Haifa

The Museum for Ethnology and Folklore in Haifa, which no longer exists in this format, was established by Dov Noy, a scholar of Jewish folk literature, who is considered one of the founders of folklore research in Israel. Even prior to the establishment of the State of Israel, Noy was one of the outstanding figures who dealt with preserving folk culture and was known mainly for his long-term project to document folktales handed down orally from generation to generation. In 1952, he participated in an international seminar devoted to the educational role of museums and as a result decided to found a folklore museum in Israel (Education Committee, 1958, 4). At that time, the mayor of Haifa, Abba Hushi, proposed to Noy to create a museum on the basis of objects donated to the city by the Israeli Ambassador to Burma, David Hacohen (for whom the Clandestine Immigration and Naval Museum in Haifa is named). Noy convinced Hushi to ascribe a more "Jewish" nature to the museum and to include in it a folktale archive. Noy hoped thereby to combine in one place "audio and visual culture" (Noy, 1977–78, 259).

The tasks of the museum, as formulated by Hushi were:

a. To save to the extent possible the nation's treasure, the greater part of which were destroyed during the Holocaust in Europe.

b. In the praiseworthy process of the ingathering of the exiles, of uprooting whole tribes from the Diaspora of Iraq, North Africa, Yemen, and so on and merging them in Israel—to take care that everything unique and characteristic about these groups will be archived and preserved for the coming generations.

c. To consolidate, as much as a poor country can, from the archives of other nations and countries so as to get to know them and have close relations with them (Education Committee, 1958, 3).

In line with these goals, the museum exhibited the ritual objects, folk art, clothing, and jewelry of the different Jewish *edot*. A collection of housewares and tools that were used by Jewish communities in the

Diaspora, as well as objects gathered from among the local non-Jewish communities (Arabs, Druze, and Circasssians) was included (Benzur, 1985). Noy's great life work is, of course, the documentation of Jewish folk literature and making it available to the public, and as part of this, he established in the museum the Folktale Archive (Noy, 1977–78). In addition, the museum dealt with the ethnography of the world's peoples, and exhibited a collection of folk art from Africa, Asia, America, and the Pacific Islands (Noy, 1963).

In 1982, the Ethnology Museum merged with the Music Museum that was located in a nearby building, and they operated jointly for a number of years. Later, both were moved to the Haifa museum compound under the administrative aegis of the new art museum (Benzur, 1985). In the 1990s the exhibition was disassembled, and the collection was moved to the warehouses of the Haifa museum authority. The collection is not offered today to the public on a permanent basis, but certain items from it are occasionally displayed in temporary exhibitions.[33]

4.d. Beit Hatfutsot—The Nahum Goldmann Museum of the Jewish People, Tel Aviv

The founding of Beit Hatfutsot can be attributed mainly to Nahum Goldmann and Abba Kovner. After the Second World War, the Lithuanian-born Goldmann became one of leaders of the Zionist movement and served for many years as the president of the World Zionist Organization and as president of the World Jewish Congress. He was professionally trained as a lawyer and historian and was one of the founders of the *Encyclopaedia Judaica* (Goldmann, 1972). Among his many endeavors, Goldmann initiated the idea of establishing a museum "that would present the Jewish Diaspora in a befitting manner" (Porat, 2000, 335).

In the mid-1960s, construction of the museum began in the Tel Aviv University compound and it was completed in 1968, before there were objects for display, and while it was still unclear what content would be exhibited in it. After many fruitless discussions, responsibility for deciding on content was given to Kovner, who had introduced a similar idea a few years earlier: to create a museum devoted to the Jewish people in the Diaspora, with the aim being to present "the world that had been destroyed and the richness of its life prior to that" (Porat, 2000, 335). Kovner was an intellectual, writer, poet, and fighter. During the Second World War, he had been a commander in the Jewish Combat Organization and led the Jewish partisan brigade in the Vilna Ghetto. In the 1948 war, he served as cultural officer of the Givati Brigade and became well known for the brigade's aggressive "battle pages." After the war, he dealt mainly with education and commemoration, being involved, among other things, in the founding of Yad Vashem as well as the Yad Mordechai Museum (Porat, 2000, 307).

Kovner worked on the plans for the Beit Hatfutsot exhibits from 1971, until the museum's opening in 1978, with numerous discussions by the museum board about them. Kovner wished to stress the suffering of the Jews in the Diaspora and the destruction wreaked upon its communities by the pogroms over the generations. That was the reason he wrote *The Scroll of Fire*—a monumental literary work comprising 52 episodes, each describing a traumatic event in the history of the Jewish people, with the idea that this composition would accompany the visitors along the exhibition (Porat, 2000, 328–36).

In contrast, the board members and other advisers felt that a focus on the suffering and destruction, if given too great a role, would cast a pall over the entire museum. They asserted that more space should be given to positive facets of the Diaspora, such as the rich spiritual life and manifestations of creativity. Goldmann, for example, envisioned two main goals for the museum. The first was "to create a living memory of the Jewish dispersal," and to illustrate to visitors "the nature and essence of the astounding phenomenon that the Diaspora embodies in the history of the Jewish people, as well as the reasons for the wondrous survival of the nation over the course of two thousand years of expulsion and oppression." The second aim was "to increase the information and deepen the understanding of the members of the young generation, who had been born in a free, sovereign state, regarding everything about the life and works of the Jews in their dispersal" (Goldmann, 1996, 2). Ultimately a compromise was reached between the two approaches, but the display was still principally based on Kovner's ideas.

The design of the Beit Hatfutsot exhibit was innovative in its time. The museum does not contain any "authentic" objects at all, but is based entirely on displays, dioramas, and reconstructed objects. The exhibit opens with a relief of the Arch of Titus, which shows the Roman victory march after the conquest of Jerusalem in 70 CE—the event marking in Jewish collective memory the beginning of the Diaspora. Then, the visitors pass through six spaces of display ("sections"), each devoted to a different aspect of life in the Diaspora: the Family Section, the Community Section, the Faith Section, the Culture Section, Among the Nations, and Return to Zion. To make it easier for visitors to understand the historical continuum, a seventh section was created, which summarizes the exhibit—the Chronosphere, in which there is a light-and-sound show about the wanderings of the Jewish people. While making their way through the linear display, from time to time the visitors pass by the "Memorial Hall," which is located in the center of the building. Standing there is a Memorial Column piercing through the three stories of the museum and constituting a monument to the Jews who were killed in the course of history for being Jewish. Displayed around the column is the work, "The Scroll of Fire."

Jesaja Weinberg, the museum's first director, explained that Beit Hatfutsot is an experiential museum, which goes beyond the accepted conventions, according to which the main role of the museum is to collect, preserve, and exhibit original objects. The reason Beit Hatfutsot does not exhibit original objects derives, he says, from the fact that the Jewish communities left behind only a few objects of "a Jewish nature," and even the existing items stem from the past three hundred years. His claim is that not enough "material remains [are available] that can reflect in a museum exhibit the essential aspects of two thousand five hundred years of Jewish life in the Diaspora" (Weinberg, 1989, 8). The reason the exhibit is arranged according to a topical cross-section, rather than in historical chronological order, as common in historical museums, derives, as he says, from the geographic dispersal of the Jewish people in the Diaspora. "The accepted chronological structure, despite ostensibly being the obvious choice in a historical museum, again does not meet the special needs of a museum dealing with the unique Jewish history" (Weinberg, 1989, 7; Nevo, 1981, 23).

Relevant for examining the ethnographic aspect is the Family Section, in which are exhibits on "the main events in the life cycle of the Jewish person, integrated within the cycle of the Jewish year—into holidays and festivals" (Rabinowitz, 1989, 9). The events and rites described in the exhibit are circumcision, bar mitzva, wedding, burial and mourning, Passover, Sukkot, Shavuot, Purim, Hanukkah, Independence Day, and Memorial Day for the Holocaust and Valor. In most instances, the customs are depicted as they were observed among Ashkenazic Jewry, and only in a few cases are the Mizrahi Jewish communities represented, as for example the Passover Seder in Spain or a circumcision in Algeria. No detailed explanation accompanies the exhibits, so that even in these two instances it is difficult to understand their "Spanishness" or "Algerianess," except for the costumes of the figures which are reminiscent of Muslim style.

FIGURE 3 | *Circumcision ceremony in Algeria, nineteenth century, Beit Hatfutsot, July 2008*

FIGURE 4 | *Passover Seder in Spain, fourteenth century,*
Beit Hatfutsot, July 2008

This was not by chance. Kovner intentionally chose to underscore the unity of the Jewish people and to that end opted to present mainly Jewish religious characteristics, with stress on the ones shared by all communities. The exhibit overwhelmingly ignores the daily life of the different communities, where the greatest differences between them are revealed. Moreover, Jewish life in the past two hundred years is not represented, including the exposure to modern influences that are not necessarily Zionist (Socialism, Communism, *Haskalah,* Assimilation); in addition, there is no representation of communities founded in the modern period in England, South America, Canada, South Africa, and Australia (Wigoder n.d.). Many claim that the result is that the museum presents a fraudulent unity: "Where are the different communities and their stories, and especially the Mizrahi and Sephardic ones? The museum is very Ashkenazic, very Eastern European" (D. Porat, 2000, 340).

Criticism was also hurled at the museum's blind adoption of the hegemonic Zionist narrative. The exhibit begins with the destruction of the Second Temple and the beginning of the Diaspora and concludes with the "Return to Zion" section, in which the *aliyot* (immigration waves) and the establishment of Israel are presented. This is an echo of the founding myth of Israeli society: Diaspora—means destruction, and establishment of the State of Israel signifies the Redemption (Shenhav-Keller, 2005, 14–15). The museum, thereby, misses its intent to commemorate the glory of the Jewish communities in the Dispersal and to celebrate their achievements there. Dafna Izraeli analyzed the museum exhibit through a gender lens, showing how, by various means, the place of women in Jewish history was ignored or marginalized both physically and symbolically (Izraeli, 1993). The epitome of the exclusion of women in the museum is expressed in the reproduction of the famous painting by Maurycy Gottlieb, *Jews Praying in the Synagogue on Yom Kippur.* In the Beit Hatfutsot version all of the women appearing in the original work have been literally erased (Lahav, 2006).

Since Beit Hatfutsot opened, the permanent exhibit has not been changed. Alongside it, temporary exhibits are mounted, usually devoted to general Jewish topics, though occasionally to a specific community. In recent years, among others, exhibits have been held on Georgian Jews (1992), Jews in Arab Countries Today (1996), Atlas Mountains Jews (1999), Synagogues in Germany (2004), Hungarian Jewry (2004), Jews in South America (2004–2005), Jewish Farmers in the Soviet Union (2006), and Jews in Melbourne (2007). Yet, these exhibitions display art works linked to the topic, but not original objects connected to the daily life of the different communities.[34]

4.e. Wolfson Museum for Jewish Art, Hechal Shlomo—Jerusalem

Inaugurated in 1958 in Jerusalem, next to the Great Synagogue on King George Street, was the "Hechal Shlomo" building, which housed the institutions of the Chief Rabbinate of Israel: the Great Rabbinic Court, the Chief Rabbinate Council, and the offices of the Chief Rabbis of Israel. That same year an exhibition of Judaica was held on the topic "From Generation to Generation." At the end of the 1960s, a museum was officially established there, as a result of a donation by Isaac and Edith Wolfson, which enabled expansion of the exhibit and acquisition of additional objects. In 1979, the museum received on long-term loan, the Arthur Hewitt collection, upon which a large part of the display is based. Over the years other collections were acquired. The museum's goal is to present a comprehensive picture of Jewish life in the various dispersals over the years, to stress the common, linking elements to the heritage of the past, as well as to serve as a monument to destroyed Jewish communities (Bialer and Fink, 1981; Inbar and Schiller, 1995, 68–69). The educational programs provided by the museum places the question of the survival of the Jewish people throughout history at the center. The answer to that question, according to the exhibition and the educational programs, is the continuous observance of Jewish culture and religion throughout the generations.

Because of the religious nature of the museum, the collection is devoted almost entirely to Judaica objects and contains mainly Jewish art and ritual objects, which had belonged to different Jewish communities around the world. Displayed alongside these items are a few local antiquities, in a way that emphasizes Jewish symbols that were maintained all through history in Jewish art. Few ethnographic items are shown in the museum; in the main, jewelry and wedding clothing from various places in the world. In addition, place is given to noting Jewish communities destroyed in the Holocaust.

FIGURE 5 | *Jewish symbols, Wolfson Museum for Jewish Art, Jerusalem, July 2008*

FIGURE 6 | *Tefillin, Wolfson Museum for Jewish Art, Jerusalem, July 2008*

4.f. Initiatives to Establish a National Museum for Jewish Edot

Despite the existence of the museums described above, there is no museum with a permanent exhibition encompassing the material and spiritual culture of all the Jewish communities. Over the years, ideas have been raised, from time to time, to found a national museum that would be devoted to Jewish life in the Diaspora and that will systematically present the diversity of the different *edot,* by stressing the ways in which they differ from each other. These initiatives arose in response to the critical reviews above of the Israel Museum, as well as of Beit Hatfutsot, which many thought was supposed to fill precisely this purpose. A notion in this spirit was raised in 1955, when the Bezalel Museum was about to undergo significant expansion. According to the plan for the enlargement, a central spot would be occupied by the Judaica department, which was supposed to cover more than one-quarter of the museum's total area. It was supposed to include three general display rooms and alongside them separate exhibition spaces for each community and ethnic group among the Jewish people (Tamir, 1990, 12). In the end, the plan was never carried out, and the Bezalel collections were transferred, as noted, to the aegis of the Israel Museum, which configured the Judaica and Ethnography wings in a different manner, as described above.

In 1993, Yossi Frost, then head of the culture section in the Ministry of Science, Culture, and Sport, referred to the problem of the small ethnic museums, which find it difficult to maintain themselves financially and have few visitors. He proposed founding a large museum, in which each community would have its own pavilion, where it could exhibit its cultural richness. Such a museum would also include communities that to this day have not established a museum. According to his recommendation, Beit Hatfutsot would remain an institution whose role would be to link each community in Israel to its counterpart abroad (Frost, 1993, 2).

Mordechai Ben-Porat, the founder of the Babylonian Jewry Heritage Museum, sees benefit in maintaining the small museums, since they enjoy the trust of the community and succeed in collecting material that a general museum has trouble receiving. Despite this, he, too, supports the approach calling for the establishment of a national museum owing to reasons connected to the completeness of the exhibition and the visitors' experience. He suggests, that "after a trial period of at least two decades of enrichment, collection, and development, the museums should be moved to Jerusalem, the capital." There, "on an area of 100 dunam … departments will be set up for the comprehensive heritage of the Jewish people with all its Eastern and Western tribes, so that the visitor will receive a whole, continuous impression" (Ben-Porat, 1993, 14–15).

In 2005, a proposal of this nature was even raised on behalf of the government. In meetings held in the Knesset following a number of private members' bills, which discussed founding national authorities for the heritage of the various *edot*, it was stated that the government had declared its intentions to establish "a National Authority for the Heritage of the Jewish *Edot*," which would encompass representation of each one of them.[35] A few months later the government backtracked from its intention because of the high cost that would be involved in carrying it out.[36] It is unclear whether the government proposal would have included the founding of a museum or only an authority that would deal solely with coordination and research. In any event the proposal came to naught.

Chapter 5

❧

Museums of the Jewish Communities

Most of the ethnographic museums in Israel dedicated to a specific ethnic group are those of Jewish communities. The Jewish *edot* are also the first to have established museums for themselves. Therefore, the first chapter describing single-ethnic-group museums is devoted to them. As noted, these initial museums were founded in the 1970s in light of the rise in inter-ethnic group tension in public discourse. The museums in this chapter appear in the chronological order of their establishment.

5.a. Museum for Yemenite Jewry Heritage of the Association for Society and Culture—Netanya

This museum, perhaps the first single-*edah* based museum in modern Israel, was established by Ovadiah Ben-Shalom, who came to Israel from Yemen in 1930, when he was seven years old. Ben-Shalom lived most of his life in Netanya and served in a number of public positions on behalf of Mapai. During his public service, he realized that Yemenite culture was gradually disappearing in the Israeli melting pot.[37] In the 1960s, Ben-Shalom initiated a Friends Circle that met weekly and held meetings Yemenite style, in which they studied Torah and conversed while smoking hookahs and chewing qat. In 1970, as a result of the circle's activity, Ben-Shalom, together with six other members, founded "The Association for Fostering Society and Culture" in a residential building in the center of Netanya.[38]

The association's activities were determined by Ben-Shalom's vision and personality and focused on linking and bridging between Jewish tradition, particularly that of Yemenite Jewry, and secular Zionist tradition. His intention was that the group's activity would be mainly devoted to the culture of Yemenite Jews, but not limited to it, and would foster other *edot*, too (Mizrahi, 2000, 76).

As soon as the Friends Circle was created, Ben-Shalom began collecting various objects related to Yemenite Jews. With the founding of the association, he decided to organize a museum in its offices, and he managed to bring this about through fundraising among the many guests from abroad who came to visit (Kesar, 18 November 2007). Since then, as time has passed, the museum has undergone many changes. Today, it occupies most of the center's area. Ben-Shalom passed away in 2004 and a memorial niche in his honor in located at the entrance to the museum. Today, the museum director is Yehiel Kesar, director of the association's office.

The museum is only one part of the association's activities, and not necessarily the part perceived as most important. The association deals with a variety of other areas, including administering the Institute for the Study of the Heritage of the Tribes of Israel, organizing conferences and seminars, and publication of the periodical *Tema* and research works. On the premises, there is also a library available for the use of scholars and the community. The association maintains contact with the members of the Yemenite emigré community and their descendants in Israel through branches throughout Israel. It encourages and nurtures musical troupes, performing artists, writers, and creative artists dealing with topics related to its activity (Mizrahi, 1997, 6–7). Special emphasis is given to activities for the community, such as scholarships for needy students, arrangement of field trips and amusement days, organization of trips abroad, and so on. In its early days, the association also engaged in nurturing family values in the spirit of Yemenite Jewry.[39]

The museum consists of many rooms, in no chronological order. The visitors pass through a series of rooms that present life in Yemen by means of objects and clothing items. The rooms are devoted to the synagogue (*al-kanis*), the room of the religious studies teacher (the *mori*), and a public sitting room in the home (the *diwan*), the kitchen, and the new mother's corner (*zawiya*).

FIGURE 7 | *The sitting room, the diwan,*
Museum for Yemenite Jewry Heritage, Netanya, Nov. 2007

The exhibition has little written explanation and no attempt was made to provide historical background for the exhibits. According to Kesar, visitors to the museum are always accompanied by a guide, who explain the meaning of the objects and their historical context (Kesar, 18 November 2007).

**FIGURE 8 | The new mother's corner, the zawiya,
Museum for Yemenite Jewry Heritage, Netanya, Nov. 2007**

5.b. The German-Speaking Jewry Heritage Museum
(The "Jeckes" Museum)—Tefen

Israel Shiloni describes in his memoirs quite picturesquely how, in 1971, he attended a conference in Jerusalem on the topic of German Jewry. He paid attention that all the Jeckes in the hall were already quite old (he himself was seventy at the time), and he was afraid lest their story be forgotten with their deaths. As an educator and man of action, he decided to found a museum in his city of Nahariya (according to him, "the only city in the world established by German Jewry") (Shiloni, 1998, 163).

After a number of pleas to the mayor of Nahariya, he was allotted a room in the municipality building, and he began to build a museum with his own hands. To be sure, Shiloni had a background in education, teaching, administration and librarianship, but he was not a historian or involved with museums. He attests about himself: "When I began to collect the material for the museum, I actually had no idea what I would exhibit there" (Shiloni, 1998, 166). Using history books, he learned about the history of German Jewry; he cut out pictures and glued them on sheets of wood purchased with his own money. He told all his acquaintances about the museum and gradually began to accumulate books and objects from estates or contributors. Shiloni took an interest in the main in collecting books written by German Jews. He amassed hundreds of such books, built shelves for them, and carried them up to the seventh story of the municipality building by himself (164–67).

FIGURE 9 | *The German-Speaking Jewry Heritage Museum, Tefen, Jan. 2007*

As time passed, the collection grew, additional volunteers joined the effort (Shiloni, too, was unpaid for this endeavor), and more and more visitors began to come to the museum, particularly Jewish emigrés and their families, and youth movement members paying a visit to Israel. In 1991, when Shiloni had reached the age of 90, he transferred the museum to the possession of Stef Wertheimer, who integrated it into the Open

Museum in Tefen, where it has remained to this day (the move was preceded by a legal dispute with the Nahariya municipality over ownership of the museum).

With the move to Tefen, Ruthie Ofek was appointed as a paid professional director, the entire collection was catalogued, the exhibition underwent comprehensive refurbishment, and the flow of visitors grew stronger. Shiloni passed away in 1996 (Shiloni, 1998, 167–76).

5.c. Old Yishuv Court Museum—Jerusalem

The Jewish population of Jerusalem has undergone many vicissitudes throughout history. In the early nineteenth century, the "Old Yishuv" of Jerusalem numbered fewer than two thousand people, most of whom were Sephardic.[40] In 1813, the Ashkenazic community in the city was renewed and organized hasidic *aliyah* from Europe to Jerusalem began. As a result, the Jewish Quarter in the Old City constantly expanded and its population became more heterogeneous (Vilnay, 1970, 356–60). One of the leaders of the rejuvenated Ashkenazic community was Rabbi Shlomo Pach Rosenthal, who lived with his family in the "Or ha-Hayyim" courtyard. This is a compound of ancient buildings, in which—according to tradition—the Ari ha-Kadosh (Rabbi Isaac Luria Ashkenazi, the greatest of the Safed mystics) was born in 1534. In the eighteenth century, Rabbi Haim Ibn Attar arrived in the courtyard from Morocco and established the Or ha-Hayyim Synagogue, which gave the court its name (Eliav, 1981, 133–35). The Pach Rosenthal family, whose members were among the leaders of the Jewish community in Jerusalem in the nineteenth century, continued to live in the court for five generations. In the 1948 war, the Jewish Quarter was destroyed, and the Pach Rosenthal family was captured along with part of the court's inhabitants (Weingarten, 1981).

At the time of the reconstruction of the Jewish Quarter after the 1967 war, it was decided to destroy a portion of the buildings and to rebuild them in a modern way, while attempting to preserve traditional construction. The structures, as well as the Or ha-Hayyim synagogue in the courtyard, were destined for razing, even though most of them were still standing. Rivka Weingarten, the granddaughter of Isaac Pach Rosenthal, who had been born and raised in the courtyard, stepped in to protect them. Weingarten decided to establish a museum there that would describe Jewish life in Old Jerusalem covering one century—from the mid-nineteenth century to the destruction of the Jewish Quarter in 1948. She turned to veteran Jerusalem families and received from them old objects for display: furniture, clothing, utensils and vessels, books, photos, and so on. To complete the collection, ritual objects were brought from ancient synagogues and traditional tools were purchased (Weingarten, 1987, 8–11; Luxembourg, 1981).

Renovation work on the structure began in the 1970s, and because of its age, the question arose of what would be the role of the building itself in the exhibit. Emphasizing preservation of the building in its original form would make it possible to demonstrate the traditional functions of different parts of the structure, such as the joint courtyard and the cistern. Conversely, the original internal division of the structure did not befit a museum, which requires large exhibition spaces, comfortable passages from room to room, gathering places for groups, and so on. Ultimately, it was decided to take a middle path—the internal arrangement of the building would be maintained as far as possible, with slight adjustments for its new purpose, and certain rooms that had historical importance were reconstructed according to their original plan. Examples of this are two synagogues—the Ari Synagogue is integrated into the exhibit and the Or ha-Hayyim Synagogue that even now serves Jewish Quarter residents for prayer services and Torah study (Gavish, 1994, 8–9; Bier,

1987). The museum was inaugurated on Jerusalem Day in 1976 and has been attracting many visitors ever since.[41]

According to Weingarten, the Old Yishuv Court Museum is not an ethnic community museum but rather one that represents "the entire spectrum of the Yishuv including all its strata and communities" (Weingarten, 1985). Daniella Luxembourg, curator of the exhibit, adds, "We had no intention of presenting each *edah* separately with its special objects and customs, but rather what they share and the residential style that was common then. The housing model we display is not relevant for all the *edot* but it does contain items that were found in every home in the quarter" (Luxembourg, 1981). At the same time, it is clear that the museum is dedicated to a very specific population with regard to ethnicity, which warrants its being included in this chapter. For example, the changes that occurred in the Jerusalem Jewish community in the nineteenth century are not described in the museum, such as the arrival of Jews from different countries, a process that resulted in a great deal of inter-community friction and finally to the splitting of the Yishuv into small ethnic *kollelim* (community or congregation of Orthodox Jews in Palestine, comprising individuals and families from a particular town or region in the Diaspora who received financial support from a *halukkah*-distribution fund).[42]

Beside the two reconstructed synagogues, the exhibit comprises residential rooms, each of which represents a different aspect of household life. The bedroom contains the bed for a new mother, wedding garb, infant care equipment, while cooking utensils are shown in the kitchen. Despite refraining from illustrating the differences between the *edot,* in general, two sitting rooms are displayed—one in the Sephardic style prevalent at the end of the Ottoman Empire and the other, in Ashkenazic style from the British Mandate period.

FIGURE 10 | *Wedding clothing and infant's cradle, Old Yishuv Court Museum, Jerusalem, February 2007). Displayed in the courtyard in the "laundry corner"*

FIGURE 11 | *Laundry niche, Old Yishuv Court Museum, Jerusalem, February 2007*

The decorative style and the ways the different rooms are arranged do exemplify the differences between the *edot*, while the radio and pendulum clock shown in the Ashkenazic room represent the technological innovations of the times. One large room shows the artisans typical of life in the quarter, such as *sofer stam* (Torah scribe), bootblack, knife sharpener, physician, spice and coffee merchant, tailor and seamstress. A recent addition is a memorial corner devoted to commemorating families from the Old Yishuv who made a special contribution to the development of certain economic branches, such as the Berman bakery, the Monson printers, and the Ginio winery.

FIGURE 12 | *Room from the Mandate period, Old Yishuv Court Museum, Jerusalem, February 2007*

5.d. Yemenite Jewish Heritage House—Rosh Haayin

In 1949–1950 the "On the Wings of Eagles" (also known as the "Magic Carpet") campaign was carried out in which almost all of Jews of Yemen were flown to Israel, about 47,000 people. Rosh Haayin was established on the ruins of a British army camp as a temporary transit camp for the immigrants. Despite the difficult conditions there, in 1951 it was declared a permanent settlement (Shimshoni, 2002, 24–25). Over the years Rosh Haayin developed and in 1994 was recognized as a city. For many years the population of Rosh Haayin remained rather homogeneous, and the veteran neighborhoods are populated to this day by emigrés from Yemen and their descendants. The creation of a homogeneous settlement enabled the preservation of the culture of Yemenite immigrants to a relatively greater extent than elsewhere, since daily contact with *olim* (immigrants) from other countries was negligible (Eliav, 1981, 192–93).

Moshe Oved, founder of the museum, began his professional path as a history teacher in Rogosin High School. Since there were no textbooks on the topic of Yemenite Jewry, Oved collected information and wrote booklets that served as the basis for study of this topic in school. As time went on, the booklets were adopted by other schools in the region, and eventually they became an information kit published by the Ministry of Education [Oved, 1981]. From the Education Ministry, Oved received photographs of the *aliyah* campaign bringing Yemenite Jews to Israel to be used in the information kit, and in 1980 he presented them in an exhibition in the school where he taught (Fenichel, 2005, 92).

As a result of the picture exhibition, work began on an "information center" on Yemenite Jewry that would mainly serve school pupils visiting from elsewhere. Oved turned to families, asking that they contribute items they had brought with them from Yemen, arranged the objects in one of the school rooms, and even wrote an information page for distribution to visitors. For some ten years Oved collected items and documents and gradually came to understand that he was essentially founding a museum, and not only an educational information center. Oved relates that he had attempted to create a place that would be a combination of the Eretz Israel Museum and Beit Hatfutsot, in the sense that it would contain both original exhibits, as well as reconstructed ones. By the mid-1990s, the museum already occupied half a floor in the school. In 1998, the school administration decided that the space was needed for classrooms and Oved was asked to transfer the exhibition to a different location (Fenichel, 2005, 92).

The museum moved to a different school and after that to the local community center. In 2005, the museum was reopened in a building in the city center, called the "Shabazi Cultural Center," where it is located today—in a structure that served the British Army until April 1948, and at the time of the immigrant camp, it was used as an infants' home (Shalev-Khalifa, 2006, 18). Posted at the entrance to the museum are explanatory signs about the historical sources of Yemenite Jewry and a map showing the concentrations of the Jewish population in Yemen. After that comes a hallway linking the three rooms of the exhibit, and on its walls is information about the immigration campaign and about Rosh Haayin in the 1950s. The first room, "the *diwan*," displays a reconstruction of a typical sitting room in a Yemenite home, with carpets, pillows for reclining, and hookahs. The second room, "The Life of a Women in Yemen," has many pieces of clothing hanging on the walls, housewares, jewelry, and mannequins representing women engaged in housework, a girl dressed in holiday garb, and an infant in a cradle. Additionally, there are signs explaining the wedding ceremony in Yemen and the daily life of Jewish women there. The third room presents the Yemenite synagogue (*al-kanis*), in which mannequins are shown representing the mori—the rabbi and religious studies teacher, and two children studying Torah. The tables hold a display of Torah scrolls and other religious works, and the wall boasts explanatory signs about spiritual and social life as well as about the Jewish community and its institutions. Another room is used as a library and lecture room.

FIGURE 13 | *The Diwan, Yemenite Jewish Heritage House, Rosh Haayin, June 2006*

FIGURE 14 | *Life of the Jewish woman, Yemenite Jewish Heritage House, Rosh Haayin, June 2006*

5.e. The U. Nahon Italian Museum of Jewish Art—Jerusalem

Italian-born Shlomo Umberto Nahon was one of the leaders of the Zionist movement before the establishment of Israel and served, among other things, as the secretary of the Histadrut in Italy and representative of the Jewish Agency (Romano, 1978, 21). After his immigration to Israel, he devoted himself to the study of Italian Jewry; he is known mainly for his efforts to bring synagogues from Italy to Israel. In the 1950s, Nahon succeeded in bringing to Israel some 40 Torah arks and Renaissance and Baroque synagogues, which had stood empty since World War II and suffered from neglect. Some of them were incorporated into synagogues in Israel, while a few became part of museum exhibitions—such as the Israel Museum in Jerusalem and the Eretz Israel Museum in Tel Aviv (Nahon, 1970).

The first synagogue brought from Italy was from the town of Conegliano Veneto in northern Italy, and it was reconstructed in its entirety in Jerusalem. The initiative for setting it up came from the Italian Jewish community in Israel, which during the Second World War had began to hold prayer services in a Jerusalem school, following the "Italian rite" (which differs from both the Ashkenazic and the Sephardic). This project received funding from the Ministry of Religions. In 1951, the first crates with parts of the synagogue arrived in Jerusalem (Nahon, 1970, 4). At Nahon's recommendation the synagogue was completely reconstructed in a hall adjacent to a school on Hillel Street,[43] with the intention being, that in the morning it would be used by the school's pupils and in the evening by the community (at that time Nahon's daughters studied in that school).

In 1952, the synagogue was opened for public use as a place of worship according to the Italian rite, and the location became the focal point of the community of Italian Jewish emigrés in Jerusalem in particular and in Israel in general. Nahon continued to import and receive various Judaica objects of Italian Jewry and began to exhibit them in a side room of the synagogue. After the school operating there moved elsewhere, and after Nahon passed away in 1974, it was decided to establish a large museum that would be named for him and preserve his project. In 1981, the museum opened, and in 1982 it was declared a recognized museum by the Ministry of Education. Today, the museum contains 1,500 items, most of them brought by Nahon himself and a few which arrived after his death. Affiliated with the museum is a research institute for Italian Jewry, as well as a center for preserving and reconstructing ancient items of wood or textiles, which carries out projects for other museum and private bodies, too. The synagogue is still active and holds regular services in which members of Jerusalem's Italian Jewish community participate.

The heart of the exhibition and its crowning glory is the synagogue itself. Alongside it, five exhibition rooms were prepared, containing hundreds of objects, mainly Judaica: Torah arks, religious works, Torah curtains (*parokhet*), synagogue furniture, charity boxes, candlesticks, Hanukkah lamps, Seder plates, chairs for the circumcision ceremony, *sukkah* parts, and so on. Among the everyday items displayed are scarves and kerchiefs, as well as a few household items (a tea service, a sewing table…). In addition to the permanent exhibit, the museum offers some seven temporary ones that change according to the annual cycle of holidays and festivals. The temporary exhibits are not shown in a separate room but items belonging to them are integrated into rooms containing the permanent exhibit. When I visited there, the exhibit was devoted to marriage and included, among other items, a *huppah* (wedding canopy) (with mannequins of a groom and bride), nineteenth-century wedding dresses, wedding rings, *ketubbot* (marriage contracts), photographs of wedding ceremonies, and a short film documenting a typical wedding of Italian Jewry.

Hanging in one of the rooms of the Italian Jewish Museum is a chart entitled "Herzl and the Zionist Movement in Italy," listing milestones in the movement's operation from 1901 to 1948. The founder of the museum, S. U. Nahon, was one of the Zionist leaders in Italy and publicized Herzl's activity in Rome. Aside from this information, the museum does not deal at all with the history of Italian Jewry. The various items displayed are presented as art objects, with their historical context not being specified. Especially striking, is the absence of reference to troubled times in the history of Italian Jewry, such as the one-hundred-and-fifty years in which Italian Jews were confined to ghettos (from the mid-sixteenth century to the end of the eighteenth), and of course, the Holocaust.

5.f. The Memorial Museum of Hungarian Speaking Jewry—Safed

The founders of the museum, Hava and Yosef Lustig, were among the leaders of the scouting youth movement "Halutzei Habonim" in Budapest and continued to deal with education after their immigration to Israel as well. In the 1980s, they thought of setting up the museum after they realized that the existing museums in Israel, and especially in Yad Vashem and Beit Hatfutsot, allotted insufficient space, as they saw it, to the story of Hungarian Jewry. They intended to prepare a small exhibit and began to spread the idea among their friends. To their surprise, their approaches received an overwhelming response, and they began to be flooded with many different kinds of materials (Y. Porat, 2006, 11–12).

FIGURE 15 | *Zionist activity in Hungary, Memorial Museum of Hungarian Speaking Jewry, Safed, January 2007*

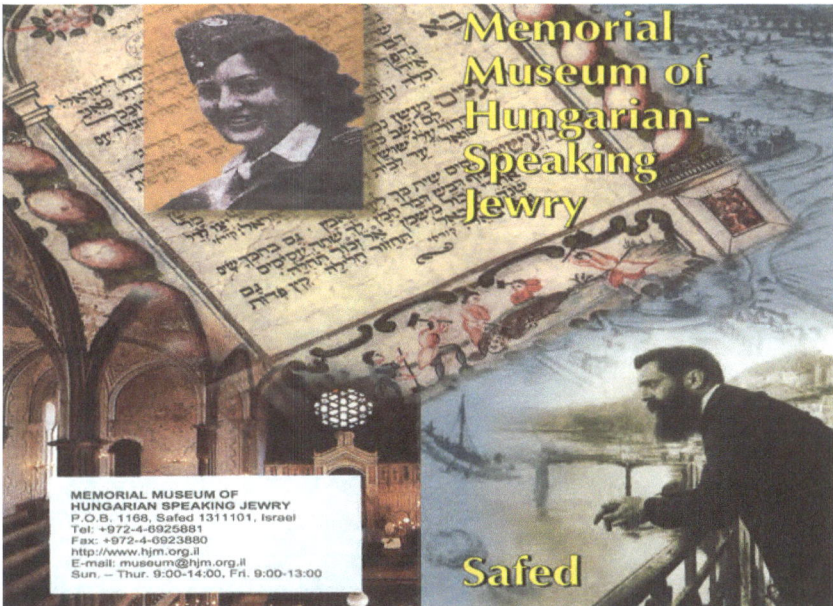

FIGURE 16 | *Bulletin of the Memorial Museum of Hungarian Speaking Jewry*

After a number of years in which many objects had accumulated, an empty Palestinian building, under the aegis of the Guardian of Absentee Property, was earmarked for the use of this project. After the building's comprehensive refurbishment, the museum was opened to the public in 1986 and continues to function today (Y. Porat, 2006, 18). As time passed, a permanent team of volunteers coalesced at the museum operating in conjunction with its salaried workers, a professional curator, the director of the guidance department, and a number of guides. Yosef Lustig still serves as the chairman of the association directing the museum. Of late, in light of the scope of the material assembled, the need to expand the museum was realized and part of the exhibition is already located in a nearby building (Lustig, 30 January 2007).

5.g. *The Museum of Jewish Heritage in Israel—Lod*

In 1981, Dr. Abraham Habermann, a librarian and scholar of medieval Hebrew literature, passed away. Habermann's student, Dr. Zvi Malachi, who directed the Lod Municipal Library, and his spouse, the late Michal Saraf, a native of Tunis, a librarian and researcher of the literature of North African Jewry, decided to establish a research institute that would be named for him.[44] This was how the Habermann Institute for Literary Research came to be; it included a rich library containing, among other things, Habermann's literature collection, as well as the Center for Oriental Jewish Culture, which publishes the journal *Mahut*, as well as books on Oriental and North African Jewry (Saraf, 1989, 37). In 1987, the museum was founded as part of the institute, which in the beginning was devoted to Tunisian Jewry— Saraf's main field of research. The idea was to show that Oriental Jewry had an impressive culture so as to elevate the group's self-confidence (Malachi, 20 August 2007).

As years passed, other ethnic communities in Lod asked for space in the museum, in order to present their cultures. To that end, community members contributed items and sometimes even entire personal collections. The museum was expanded to include additional Mizrahi Jewish ethnic groups, and finally became the Museum of Jewish Heritage in Israel. According to Malachi, "Whoever contributes—is represented. Whoever does not contribute is not represented." The Bulgarian community was very involved in setting up the exhibit, but in the meantime has practically disappeared from the city. In contrast, Malachi says the Ethiopian community scarcely showed any interest in the museum and the exhibits in the room devoted to Ethiopia did not originate with the local community (and Malachi says that most of the items have no actual historical or cultural value). The most involved communities today are those stemming from India and from Russia (Malachi, 20 August 2007).

The museum has rooms arranged around a circular courtyard, linked by a corridor. Each room is devoted to a different community. Displayed in the largest room, dedicated to North African Jewry, are a wedding gown from Tunis, other holiday garb, housewares, and many Judaica objects (menorahs, marriage contracts, and the like). Presented in the room devoted to Indian Jewry are dozen of mannequins demonstrating Jewish rites as performed in the various Indian communities (engagement, wedding, child rearing), as well as ancient books and traditional Indian costumes. Shown in the rooms devoted to the Jewries of Bukhara and Bulgaria are clothing, housewares, kitchen utensils, and photographs. The Ethiopian room displays cooking utensils, various photographs and documents related to the campaign of their *aliyah* to Israel. A number of rooms are devoted to unique collections donated by people from Eastern Europe, such as Passover *Haggadot,* a number of statuettes presenting Jews in the Eastern European shtetl as well as an exhibition of miniature models of synagogues in Poland made out of matches and wooden strips, including synagogues that were destroyed in the Holocaust. The corridor displays items from Russian Jewry, mainly uniforms and medals from immigrants who served in the Red Army in World War II.[45]

Easily discernible is that this is a varied collection, with each item coming from a different source, and that the manner of presentation is dictated by the objects donated by the various communities. Over the years there was no guiding hand fashioning a uniform image for the museum, and each room is designed in a different manner. In a few rooms, the objects are arranged in display cases; in others, they are placed on the floor, gathering dust and suffering from severe neglect. The museum does not have many local visitors, and most of its income comes from organized groups. To strengthen the link to the local community, folklore evenings are held in the museum under the title of "A Museum Sings and Tells about Heritage," each time dedicated to a different ethnic group.[46]

5.b. Babylonian (Iraqi) Jewry Heritage Museum—Or Yehuda

Between 1949 and 1952, as part of the "Ezra and Nehemiah" campaign, some 122,000 *olim* came to Israel from Iraq—a greater number of immigrants than from any other country in that period (D. Hacohen, 1994, 323–25). The wave of mass immigration led to the establishment of five *ma'barot* (transit camps) on the ruins of the Arab villages of Saqiya, Kafr 'Ana, and Kheiriya. A few years later, the *ma'barot* were declared as the Or Yehuda local council. Counter to Jewish Agency policy, the Iraqi immigrants did not agree to move to agricultural settlements in the periphery and tenaciously requested to remain in transit camps in the center of Israel, while immigrants from other countries left them. That explains why Or Yehuda became the only place in Israel where the majority of the population was from Iraq, a situation that remained unchanged until the beginning of the 1980s (A. Cohen and Katan, 1966, 13–17; Ben-Yaakov, 1980, 307).

Mordechai Ben-Porat, founder of the center and the museum, began his public career as an emissary for the "Mosad le-Aliyah Bet" (organization for illegal immigration) in Baghdad, where he was responsible for organizing the Iraqi Jews for the Ezra and Nehemiah immigration campaign.[47] From 1955 to 1969, he was the head of the Or Yehuda local council and was considered a very dominant council head, who was well connected to the national political institutions and working assiduously to reinforce the "local consciousness" of the residents (A. Cohen and Katan, 1966, 50–51). To be sure, Ben-Porat did indeed originate in Iraq, but by virtue of his public functions one may consider him part of the absorbing establishment. He claims that in Israel there is discrimination based on ethnic origin, but it is neither systematic nor intentional, as others argue. He thinks that it is possible to promote the Mizrahi Jews in Israel by disseminating their heritage and bringing it to public awareness through institutions of education and the media (Ben-Porat, 1980, 26).

From the mid-1960s through the mid-1980s, Ben-Porat served on and off as a Knesset member on behalf of the Rafi, Labor, Telem, and Likud parties, and even served as a Minister-without-portfolio in the Begin and Shamir governments. In 1973, as a Knesset member, Ben-Porat established the Babylonian Jewry Heritage Center Association in Or Yehuda and from then on served as its chairman (Ben-Yaakov, 1980, 453–54). This was a period in which the inter-ethnic tension in Israel had already broken out and could not be denied—two years after the start of the activity of the Black Panther movement in Jerusalem. Situated at the heart of the political establishment and Zionist endeavor, Ben-Porat took care that the founding of the center not be perceived as a divisive move that would increase the tension. Ben-Porat used his political power in Or Yehuda and initiated a decision, whereby the local council would allot a plot of land for free "to whoever wishes to erect a building for the preservation of their community's heritage" (Ben-Porat, 1993, 34). He consistently presents the Iraqis as the first *edah* to make use of this opportunity and to establish the heritage center, even though the process was actually the opposite (Meir-Glitzenstein, 2004, 189).

At the ground-breaking ceremony for the center, Ben-Porat stressed his dedication to state values over-arching all communities. He suggested that other *edot* take part in the work of the center and declared that its various institutions "will not be solely for Iraqi immigrants, but will encompass the entire gamut of the Jewish people, since we maintain that the Iraqi heritage is not only that of the Babylonian Jews, but of the entire Jewish world."[48] Even the name of the museum fits in well with the effort to create a display of unity. The choice of the term "Babylonian Jewry," instead of "Iraqi Jews," blurs the Arab identity of the country of origin, as well as the Arab identity of the immigrants themselves. Moreover, opting for the biblical term "Babylonia" reflects an attempt to forge a link to the all-Jewish ethos of Babylonian exile, thereby bringing the entire nation under the wings of the museum. Concealed beneath the surface is the premise that the Jews who lived in Iraq in the twentieth century were the direct descendants of the biblical Babylonian exiles, a belief accepted among Iraqi Jewry, but disputed among historians.[49]

Construction of the center's large building was completed in 1977, on the city's main street (then Haganah Street; now Mordechai Ben-Porat Street). The site selected is adjacent to the memorial commemorating the Zionist movement activists who were hanged in Iraq, Yosef Basri and Shalom Salah; it, too, was erected at Ben-Porat's initiative.[50] The center began with the organization of research activity, arranging historical conferences, and publishing periodicals and books on the history of Iraqi Jewry. Professionals were hired to plan the museum and its display. Prof. Yitzhak Avishur, who chaired the academic staff, related that the collecting of the objects for exhibit began in 1976. Many people considered the future museum as a kind of home for the display of objects, implements, and clothing of Iraqi Jewry, but after discussions were held, his approach was accepted, namely, that the museum had to be an institution with a more academic nature. Thus, it was decided to exhibit not only objects and implements, but also orderly historical information, accessible to the public and based on studies on the history of Babylonian Jewry. The academic work that preceded the founding of the museum included carrying out a comprehensive survey of Iraqi immigrants in Israel, with the aim of collecting objects and stories, as well as photographing items whose owners were not willing to part with them. This stage was implemented under the guidance of Aviva Muller-Lancet, the curator of the ethnography wing of the Israel Museum. Towards the reconstruction of the Great Synagogue of Baghdad for the center, Iraqi immigrants who remembered the structure were interviewed, and their recollections were examined by architect David Cassuto. In addition, the founding staff visited museums abroad with the aim of garnering ideas.[51]

The museum was inaugurated in 1988, at a large ceremony attended by an audience of thousands, in the presence of the President of Israel, the Minister of Education, and the Speaker of the Knesset. At this occasion, Ben-Porat declared that the museum meshes well with the spiritual-cultural climate in Israel, which grants greater legitimacy to cultural difference (Medad, 1988, 14). In time, many donations of objects were received, and the collection had expanded to thousands of items by 1991 (Sharoni, 1991, 13; Yehuda, 1991, 16–17). New wings were dedicated in the permanent exhibition and thematic temporary exhibits were offered (Yehuda, 1990, 30–31; Sharoni, 1990, 31; Yehuda, 1992, 9–10). In 1999, the center underwent extensive refurbishment, as part of which the exhibit was doubled in area and content and took on its current form ("Dream and Its Realization" 1999, 27–32). From its establishment through today, the Museum of Babylonian Jewry has maintained its standing as one of the largest ethnographic museums in Israel, perhaps the largest of all, regarding both the size of its collection and display as well as the number of visitors, which comes to over ten thousand per year. An educational department is active on site, operating a team of guides, developing educational programs for different ages, and marketing them to schools and kindergartens throughout Israel (Atar, 1991, 11–12; Shaham, 2005, 47). Moreover, the team involved in the founding of the museum, as described above, was exceptional in its size compared to other museums, which were established typically by one or two persons.

The dedication of the museum founders to official Zionist values is reflected not only in the symbolic components surveyed above, but is explicitly expressed also in the content. The entry sign to the museum presents the frame story: "Displayed in this museum is a small exhibit of the splendor of Babylonian Jewry from ancient times through today; from the time when the eternal oath was sworn by the rivers of Babylon, 'if I forget thee, O Jerusalem, let my right hand forget her cunning,' to its *aliyah* to the State of Israel." The first display rooms of the exhibit are devoted to the history of the Jewish community in Iraq, but the exhibit skips over hundreds of years of history and "jumps" from the Geonic period directly to modern times. For example, in the wing devoted to education, the types of yeshivot from the Talmudic and Geonic periods are described and immediately followed by the educational institutions of Alliance Israélite Universelle established at the end of the nineteenth century. The yeshivot from the modern period and the important rabbis who headed them receive scant mention.

FIGURE 17 | *Swearing-in ceremony of new members of the Haganah*

The museum pays a great deal of attention to Zionist activity in Iraq, in the form of an entire wing called "Zionism and Aliyah." Actually this is the only wing describing in great detail the historical processes that Iraqi Jews underwent in the modern period. This creates an (incorrect) impression, as if all that engaged the Iraqi Jewish population in the first half of the twentieth century was "Zionism and Aliyah," and a bit of European education and western sports (displayed before this). Presented at the start of this wing are the pioneering youth movements in Iraq in the 1930s. Then, the activities of the Zionist Hehalutz movement are described, organized by emissaries of Aliyah Bet (illegal immigration) and the Jewish Agency. As previously mentioned, the founder of the museum, Mordechai Ben-Porat, belonged to this movement prior to his immigration to Israel). Special attention is given to the story of those executed in Iraq for Zionist activity—Yosef Basri and Shalom Salah—near whose commemorative monument the museum was built, as noted above.

FIGURE 18 | *Sukkot festival following the customs of Babylonian Jewry*

"The Emissaries," organizers of *aliyah* on behalf of Israel, which were led by Ben-Porat, were allotted a memorial wall, which displays a photo and basic biographical details of each of the 25 emissaries, one of whom was a woman. This distinguished and detailed presentation of the emissaries stresses Israel's activity in Iraq and emphasizes the lack of a display of local leadership. Rabbis and intellectuals, such as the hundreds of local youths who contributed to the organization of the emigration as well as the activists in the "breakaway" movements (Betar, Etzel, Lehi), receive marginal mention, if at all. Obviously, there is no sign of those Iraqi Jews who did not subscribe to the Zionist ideology, but rather supported integration within the Arab society in Iraq, even though the proportion of educated Jews was higher among them than among the Zionists (Meir-Glitzenstein, 2004, 192–95).

A special place in the Zionism and Aliyah wing is devoted to the "Farhud"—the 1941 riots against the Iraqi Jews in which some two hundred Jews were killed over two days. Since these pogroms took place during the Second World War, inspired by a pro-Nazi revolution that had occurred in Iraq a short time before, many people, including President Itzhak Ben-Zvi, suggested considering the Farhud as part of the Holocaust story. This recommendation was accepted, because it fit in well with attempts to ascribe to the Holocaust a national dimension and to include in it the story of as many non-European communities as possible as well as with efforts to foster the ethos of the Arab-Nazi link. The Iraqi Jews, who initially perceived the Holocaust as a narrative solely of European Jews, understood that including them in the story of the Holocaust provided them with political clout in Israel. So, from the 1980s on, they also began to consider the Farhud as part of the Holocaust (Jablonka, 2008, 228–38). Presenting the Farhud in the museum of Iraqi Jewry definitely illustrates this by making use of the accepted methods of commemoration at Yad Vashem, for example, by calling those who save Jews during the Farhud "Righteous Among the Nations" (Meir-Glitzenstein, 2004, 193).[52]

Following that, the Ezra and Nehemiah campaign is described in the form of photos of *olim* in Iraq, on airplanes on the way to Israel, and at the Lod airport. The final section of the Zionism and Aliyah wing is devoted to the beginning of life in Israel. First comes the depiction of life in *ma'barot* (immigrant transient camps) and then the immigrants' integration into the agricultural settlement endeavor in Israel, in preparatory groups, in self-supporting settlement, in kibbutzim and moshavim. Noticeable here, too, is an intentional embellishment of historical reality. Iraqi Jewry, who were overwhelmingly urban, followed a modern way of life, and inexperienced in agricultural, tenaciously insisted upon arriving in Israel to settle in the large, well-established cities in the center of Israel, especially in Tel Aviv and its suburbs. In contrast to *olim* from other Arab countries, most of the Iraqi immigrants actively opposed government policy and did not agree to move from the temporary transit camps in the central region to agricultural settlements in the periphery. Against this backdrop, a serious rift developed between the immigrants and the establishment for absorbing them. The *olim* lost faith in the establishment and held strikes and violent demonstrations. The government, on its part, considered them a most problematic immigrant group and hastened to suppress what it defined as "a rebellion with a political tinge" (Meir-Glitzenstein, 2000, 278–94).

Of these harsh events, of course, no mention is made in the museum, but the contrary—the photos display precisely those isolated instances in which the Iraqi immigrants did become part of agricultural settlement (on the whole, these are Kurdish Jews, and not the "Babylonians"). This decision is especially striking in light of the placement of the museum, the city of Or Yehuda, whose very existence is a living monument to the struggles of the Iraqi immigrants. The city's beginnings were in five temporary transit camps whose inhabitants, mostly from Iraq, did not agree to leave. Gradually, "squatters" came to them—Iraqi emigés who had left settlements in the periphery to which they had been sent and who preferred to live illegally in transit camps in the center of Israel (Glitzenstein, 2000, 284–85). The five transit camps united and were declared, with no other choice, as a permanent urban settlement and in opposition to the government decision to preserve the rural-agricultural nature of the region (E. Cohen and Katan, 1966, 13–15). The Museum of Babylonian Jewry does not deal with the local history of Or Yehuda, thereby skipping over this problematic chapter, in which the Iraqi immigrants rebelled against the Zionist establishment (of which Ben-Porat was a part).

5.i. Cochin Jewish Heritage Center—Nevatim

Moshav Nevatim near Beersheba was established in 1946 as part of the "11 points" in the Negev and was settled by various groups of immigrants who abandoned it one after the other owing to difficulties of adjustment. Around 1954 Jews from the Cochin Principality in the Indian state of Kerala immigrated to Israel; they were distributed among a number of moshavim around Israel, including Nevatim. Over the course of two decades, the Cochin Jews succeeded in turning this agricultural settlement into one of the most flourishing in Israel, and until today, most of the families in Nevatim have their origin in Cochin (Shahar and Cacen, 2008, 127). In recent years, the profitability of some branches of agriculture has declined, and the moshav members have begun to develop other channels of income, among them internal tourism, by renting out apartments and vacation rooms and the establishment of restaurants serving Indian food. This was the backdrop also for the development of the Cochin Jewry Heritage Center.

The idea was born in 1984, following a temporary exhibit held by Cochin Jews on the thirtieth anniversary of their *aliyah* to Israel. This exhibition made many of them aware that the heritage they had brought with them from India was gradually disappearing with the passing away of the older generation. After the temporary exhibit had been dismantled, Yitzhak Eliya decided that if objects would not be collected now, they would be lost, so he initiated the founding of the museum together with a number of friends. They began to collect items and information about the history and customs of the *edah*. At the same time Eliya established an association and managed to obtain funding from the local council and the Ministry of Education. A small, temporary exhibit was set up in two rooms in the old gymnasium in the center of the moshav. After objects and information had been accumulated, Eliya turned to the Israel Museum, since he wanted to establish a museum that would meet professional standards and be able to turn into a recognized museum. With the intercession of the Israel Museum, professionals were hired to design the exhibit and the museum, which also includes a synagogue, was officially opened in 1995 (Fenichel, 2005, 122–25).

FIGURE 19 | *The Wedding, Cochin Jewish Heritage Museum, Nevatim, June 2006*

Eliya says that the museum is intended first of all for the young people of the moshav, so they can learn about their historical heritage and to urge them to preserve certain elements and not be totally assimilated into Israeli culture. Other aims are to raise the status of the small community in the eyes of Israeli society and of course to draw Israeli and foreign tourists to the moshav. The future plan is to integrate the museum into a larger tourism project that will also include a Cochin house, a performance hall, a building for holding workshops, a tropical garden, stores, and a restaurant, all in Cochin style—a kind of Indian street for tourists in Israel (Fenichel, 2005, 130–34).

FIGURE 20 | *Holiday and Festival Clothing,*
Cochin Jewish Heritage Museum, Nevatim, June 2006

5.j. *The Worldwide North Africa Jewish Heritage Center —*
Jerusalem

The Jews of North Africa (the Maghreb—Morocco, Tunisia, and Algeria) began to settle in Jerusalem in the 1830s, and their community continuously grew, even though it was very poor. Organizationally and economically, it was affiliated with the large, well-established, *Kollel ha-Edah ha-Sepharadit,* despite its actually being distinct from the Sephardim in customs, language, and culture. The Maghreb representatives claimed that they were disadvantaged by the Sephardim in the allotment of the *Halukah* money.[53] In 1854, Rabbi David ben Simon (acronym: Devash) arrived in Jerusalem from Morocco and six years later he established the "Committee of the Edah ha-Moghrabit," thereby disconnecting the Maghrebi Jews from the Edat ha-Sefardim and turning it into an independent *edah* (Kark 1991, 66–83). Between 1866 and 1868 the committee founded the Mahane Israel neighborhood, the first Jewish neighborhood outside the walls of the Old City that was built by residents of the city and at their initiative.[54]

The neighborhood was called the Moghrabi neighborhood by its inhabitants, but Mamila by others (owing to its proximity to the Mamila Pool). Over the years, the neighborhood residents suffered many hardships, its houses were crowded and neglected, and the neighborhood was even abandoned and resettled a number of times. Even before the 1948 war, the neighborhood was swallowed up among the other houses in the New City and its identity as an independent neighborhood was forgotten. As a result of the war, it almost completely emptied out because of its proximity to the municipal boundary line— the border line (Hazan 2001, 9–13). After the 1967 war, the area was resettled, but the Mahane Israel neighborhood, with its geographical isolation and its ethnic character, was lost.

One of the first buildings erected in the Mahane Israel neighborhood was the Kollel, in which was housed the *beit midrash* (study hall) and shelter for the poor, homeless people of the community (today 13 Moghrabim St.). In the 1980s, at the initiative of the chairman of *Edah* Committee Akiva Azoulai, it was decided to renovate the building and to situate in it the Worldwide North Africa Jewish Heritage Center.[55] The last residents were vacated in 1988, and the planning stages and fundraising were conducted by

David Susannah, who was appointed chairman of the center's board. The center's budget was provided mainly by donations from wealthy members of the *edah* located outside of Israel (Gozlan, 31 Jan. 2007; M. Hacohen 1989, 26; Gian 2000, 22).

According to the architect in charge of the renovation works, essential questions about preservation of the heritage were posed as early as the initial planning stages. The founders considered the issue of what type of character should be given to the structure: whether to refurbish it in the spirit of the heritage of North Africa, which the Jews had left behind, or in that of the Jerusalem heritage at the end of the nineteenth century, when the neighborhood of which the building is a historical remnant was built and populated. The decision was to use both of them, preserving the outward appearance of the old

building, so as to maintain the original character of the neighborhood, yet to change the internal design of the building entirely. To give expression to the material world in which the Jews of North Africa had lived, magnificent architectural elements in traditional Moroccan style were incorporated into the building, which were specially created by artisans brought to Israel from Morocco for that purpose.

FIGURE 21 | *Worldwide North Africa Jewish Heritage Center, Jerusalem, Jan. 2007*

Their particular pride is the patio—the entrance hall to the building, which is decorated with luxurious stucco work and arches bearing geometric patterns and inscriptions in Moroccan and Andalusian style (Hazan, 2001, 11–13).

Most of the objects at the Center were acquired in Morocco especially for the exhibit and are not necessarily "Jewish," that is, they were not made by Moroccan Jews or used by them. Sometimes items are received from members of the community after they visit and see the Heritage Center. The Moroccan exhibit, for example, was donated by a Jew who had set it up in his home and then decided some time later to sell it. Today, the Center's director is Avraham Gozlan, who had previously worked in the Jewish Agency in the absorption of North African immigrants. The Center has become a lodestone for North African Jews in Israel. The elders of the community who come to Jerusalem to visit the Western Wall visit the Center afterwards and "return to their roots." Gozlan is proud that the Jerusalem members of the community attend events held at the Center, but not events organized in their neighborhoods. Another widespread custom is to conclude bar mitzvah celebrations held at the Western Wall in the Center. The Center's synagogue is not active on a regular basis, but is used as such for events.

The catalog published on the occasion of the opening of the permanent exhibition, which memorialized 51 central figures in the history of Moroccan Jewry, states that the Center "will serve not only as a museum, presenting pictures of the past, but also as a source of inspiration and a driving, motivating force, and this magnificent building will become a lively place for anyone thirsting for information, people of all ages and from all communities, from Israel and throughout the world," and moreover, "the intention was to create a spirited cultural center that would serve as a focal point for study, research, and consideration, for exhibits and exhibitions, for lectures and conferences, for an archive and repository, for folklore events and to preserve and commemorate the roots of North African Jewry" (Toledano, 2005, 5).

Indeed, the Center serves not only as a museum, but hosts various cultural activities. It conducts a course in *piyyut* in the style of Moroccan Jewry as well as an institute for training *Hazzanim*. A reception hall was built on the second floor (Gozlan, 31 Jan. 2007). In 2005, the museum mounted an exhibition presenting a selection of paintings by "Tunisian trend" painters in modern art (Rubinstein-Cohen, 2005). In 2006, the Center hosted Mimouna celebrations, which included a concert of music and *piyyut,* and a seminar on customs for the day after Passover. The purpose of the event was to confront the "low" folk image of the Mimouna celebrations and to raise the related customs from the status of folklore to that of culture (Ettinger, 21 April 2006).

FIGURE 22 | *Moroccan wedding dress, Worldwide North Africa Jewish Heritage Center, Jerusalem, Jan. 2007*

The exhibit is spread over a number of stories and includes mainly three kinds of objects: display mannequins, mainly feminine, dressed in traditional garb; cooking implements typical of the region; and posters with historical information about North African Jewry. The historical information focuses on the link with Holy Land Jewry, particularly with migration to Israel after the Second World War. Zionist activity prior to the war is mentioned, but not as extensively described as the waves of immigration after it. There is a historical reason for that: though the Zionist movement was active in North Africa, until the Second World War it was not very successful and sufficed with fundraising more than encouraging *aliyah* (Abitbol, 1981, 119–29). The museum does provide information about the difficulties of Libyan Jewry under Italian rule, in brief, but does not mention anti-Semitism or problems elsewhere. For example, the anti-Semitic harassment of Algerian Jews at the end of the nineteenth century is not noted (Abitbol, 113).

5.k. Museum of Libyan Jews—Or Yehuda

The Jewish community of Libya was in continuous existence from the sixteenth century on, mainly around Tripoli. After the establishment of the State of Israel, almost all Libyan Jews immigrated to it, some thirty thousand people.[56] In the 1980s, the World Organization of Libyan Jews was founded as a framework confederating within it organizations and associations working for the Libyan Jews in Israel. At the end of the 1990s, the need arose to build a large center for the organization, and an idea was promoted to found a museum representing the community as well. The organization's chairman, Rami Cahalon, turned to Avi Pedazur, a member of the community who was a Lieutenant-colonel in the Air Force, with a request to take on the project of establishing the museum; Pedazur had previously planned the Air Force Museum at Hazerim. He visited Beit Hatfutsot and asserted that he found no material on Libyan Jewry, which goaded him to devote himself to founding the museum. In 2000, Pedazur began the collection of material. Together with a team of volunteers, he scoured the country and amassed material from community members, including thousands of photos (he is proud that "the Libyan Jews are the most photographed community in Israel"). Yet, he also felt it was important to obtain many original objects from Libya and not to suffice with photos and reconstructions (Pedazur, 20 June 2006).[57]

In 2000, the organization received an old building, previously serving as a community center, located in the heart of a neighborhood in which many residents are of Libyan origin, and renovation works were started and the establishment of the museum began. The structure had been put at the disposition of the organization with the help of the then mayor of Or Yehuda, Yitzhak Bokovza, whose family had immigrated from Libya, who made use of the city ordinance initiated in 1973 by Mordechai Ben-Porat that allowed every *edah* to receive an area from the Or Yehuda municipality for a heritage center. Though the museum opened unofficially as early as 2002, work on it has actually never ceased, and as of this writing, it has not been officially inaugurated. Despite that, the museum is active and welcomes visitors, who hear about the place by word of mouth. Many events and receptions are held there on behalf of the Libyan Jewry organization and the association itself brings official guests there from Israel and abroad for guided tours; also active on site is an institute for the study of and research into Libyan Jewry (Pedazur, 20 June 2006).[58]

Pedazur designed the exhibition as he saw fit, and he tells that from the outset he accepted the task of establishing the museum on the condition that he was to be given a free hand in designing it. The main, declared goal of the museum, as he sees it, is to stress the fact that the story of Libyan Jewry is parallel to, even identical with, the story of the State of Israel. He considered it essential not to create a "weepy Mizrahi museum," as he puts it, but to present the fate shared with Zionism and the State of Israel, through the link to Judaism. He adds, "This is the first time that Mizrahi Jews are not setting up an anthropological museum, but an Israeli one." In order to attract young people to the site, he felt it important that the museum not deal only with the past, but also with the present and future. To that end, the display does not end with the arrival of Libyan Jews in Israel, but continues through to today and includes the life of Libyan Jews in Israel (see the ensuing in the description of the exhibit). He perceives the museum as dynamic and includes the life of Libyan Jews in Israel, in line with historical developments (if you visit it in a hundred years perhaps there will be a pavilion about Libyan Jews and extraterrestrials) (Pedazur, 20 June 2006).

Zionism is palpable in almost every nook and cranny of the museum. To begin with, in the entrance plaza an Israeli flag is flying, and another flag is inside, in the entrance hall. The colors blue and white also dominate the museum's logo and its guidance signs. The museum is relatively large and comprises several exhibition spaces.[59] The entry sign offers a concise history of Libyan Jewry, from its beginnings to the exodus of the Jews. The exhibit itself begins in the "Zionism Pavilion," which starts with a description of the start of Zionism in Libya, in the form of an exchange of letters between Herzl and the community in the years 1900 to 1904. Most of the area of the main hall is dedicated to the activity of the Zionist movement in Libya, by topic: *hachsharot* (agricultural preparatory camps), illegal immigration to Israel, the Haganah, youth movements, and the modern educational system. For each topic there is a pithy explanation and many photos, along with a plethora of Zionist symbols, such as: Shields of David, blue Jewish

National Fund collection boxes, quotations from the Declaration of Independence, and the like.

The visitors then enter the "Pavilion of Aliyah to the Land of Israel," which displays many items concerned with the establishment of the State of Israel, not necessarily linked to Libyan Jewry. For example, under the title of "Revival" a newspaper from the day the State of Israel was established is presented, a copy of the Declaration of Independence, pictures of Herzl and Ben-Gurion

FIGURE 23 | *Revival, Museum of Libyan Jews, Or Yehuda, June 2006*

Opposite this wall is the figure of a farmer at work, and alongside it agricultural implements and work tools. This corner is reminiscent of a typical display in museums on the history of Zionist settlement. The only thing making this Libyan is the dedication of part of it to commemorate the work of Avigdor Raccah, the most active figure among the community leaders who dealt with the absorption of the mass *aliyah* in the early years of the State of Israel. Tomer Katriel claims that the museums on the history of settlement constitute focal points for pilgrimage by secular "pilgrims" of Ashkenazic background (Katriel,

1997, 73). Reproduction of the agricultural display in a museum of an *edah* that is not Ashkenazic, and for the most part not secular, makes use of the pioneering ethos and makes it part of the Libyan Jewish community, so as to give prominence to its central role of in the heart of Israeli Zionist society.[60]

FIGURE 24 | A farmer, Museum of Libyan Jews, Or Yehuda, June 2006

A special corner is devoted to the "Hebrew woman and mother in Libya," in which the role of women in the family and in community life is described as well as the changes that have taken place in the life of women in Libya in the past one hundred years, owing to the feminist revolution —and especially to the organizations that arose from the end of the nineteenth century to the beginning of the twentieth, whose aim was advancement of women's standing and encouragement of women's leadership. The exhibit commemorates in a special way four women who were involved in public activity in Libya and continued their endeavors after immigrating to Israel, presenting an explanation about each one of them, in addition to personal items of each. Adjacent to this is a spot for "spiritual heritage in Libya," devoted to the endeavors of the community's rabbis throughout history, and particularly in recent times; on display are portraits of dozens of the community's rabbis and spiritual leaders. Here, too, the "Zionist perspective" is not missing, and in the explanatory sign emphasis is placed on the contribution of the rabbis to Zionist activity: to illegal immigration, the Haganah, and *aliyah*. Likewise, shown are mannequins representing a couple's marriage ceremony and a boy's bar mitzvah rite.

FIGURE 25 | *The Yizkor Pavilion, Museum of Libyan Jews—*
Or Yehuda, June 2006

Next to the main hall is a room called "The Yizkor Pavilion," in which the Holocaust of Libyan Jewry is memorialized as well as the anti-Jewish riots that took place in 1945, 1948, and 1967. During the Second World War, Libya was under Italian rule, and the Libyan Jews suffered from the Italian racial laws; a few hundred were murdered in concentration camps in Libya and Europe. The Libyan Jews struggled for recognition by Israel's state memorializing institutions, as victims of the Holocaust and also for being included among those receiving compensation under the Reparations Agreement (Jablonka, 2008, 252–55). The room contains a model of the Libyan Jadu concentration camp, whose survivors were the only emigrés from Libya recognized by the official institutions as Holocaust survivors, even though there were other camps whose prisoners suffered just as well (Jablonka, 2008, 255).

The room does not commemorate Jews murdered in anti-Semitic riots and events that preceded the Holocaust, although happenings such as these are mentioned elsewhere in the museum. The exhibit thereby creates a conscious link between victims of the Holocaust and victims of the riots related to the history of the State of Israel, similar to the hegemonic Zionist narrative, which presents the establishment of the State as a necessary and inevitable result of the Holocaust.

After the Yizkor Pavilion the exhibit reaches the heights of patriotism, in the "*Oz u-Mofet* [Strength and Model Behavior] Pavilion," devoted to Libyan Jews who served, and are serving, in the Israel Defense Forces (the pavilion is essentially a hallway linking the two parts of the museum, so visitors have to pass through it). Alongside enlarged models of medals of valor, strength, and model behavior hang the flags of the various IDF army corps and on the opposite wall hang photographs received from the Army Spokesman's Film Unit. The explanation accompanying the pictures describes the contribution of Libyan immigrants to the War of Independence and notes sixteen soldiers of Libyan origin who were killed in the war. The texts are written in heroic language, full of pathos, as for example in the following: "Imbued with nationalism, suffused with Zionist consciousness, replete with Hebrew education, the graduates and members of pioneering youth movements, some familiar with weaponry from their youth in Libya, they were willing to take on any mission and any challenge, faithfully and devotedly, enthusiastically and joyfully, demonstrating bravery and self-sacrifice, for the homeland."

On the lower level, a marketplace is depicted with its different types of tradesmen and craftsmen: a tailor, a barber, spice seller, and so on. The exhibit contains dozens of original objects and vessels, with no explanation being given. The last room in the museum is devoted to current art and displays works by artists of Libyan origin living in Israel. This gives expression to Pedazur's vision for creating a museum that will be relevant for young members of the *edah*. The room is called "The Generation of the Future Draws the Generation of the Past" (Pedazur, 20 June 2006).

5.l. The Children of the Bible (Karaite Judaism) Heritage Museum—Jerusalem

Karaite Judaism is an *edah* founded in Babylonia in the eighth century that gradually separated from the institutions of mainstream Judaism—Rabbinic Judaism. The Karaites are distinguished from the rabbinic stream by a variety of customs and traditions, with the basis of their faith being only in the Written Scripture (the Bible) and rejection of the Oral Law. This explains the derivation of their various appellations, all approximately meaning "scripturalist": *ba'alei mikra, benei mikra,* or *kara'im.*[61] The Karaite community in Jerusalem has always been very small and included a synagogue apparently built in the Middle Ages (Karaite tradition sets its construction in the eighth century, and a few buildings around it that were handed down by legacy from generation-to-generation. The location, which gained the name of "the Karaite court," is located on Karaite Street, opposite the ruins of the Tiferet Israel Synagogue. The Karaite court was destroyed in the 1948 war, together with the entire Jewish Quarter, and with it the Karaite community of Jerusalem, which then numbered fewer than twenty people (Vilnay, 1970, 428–32).

Upon the establishment of the State of Israel, a large Karaite community immigrated to it from Egypt and made their home in a number of cities and settlements in southern and central parts of Israel, especially around the city of Ramleh, where the center of Karaite Judaism is located today. After the 1967 war, the Jerusalem synagogue was renovated as part of the reconstruction program for the Jewish Quarter. The Karaite community hoped it would be able to renew the Karaite community on site, but the company for development of the quarter settled Orthodox families there (Elgamil, 1979, 253). In 1978, the community's Council prepared the synagogue anew for prayer services and put in charge of it Rabbi Moshe Dabah and his family, who live in the apartment above the synagogue. Many members of the Karaite community come to pray there on the Sabbath and holidays (Dabah, 28 May 2008).

Since this synagogue is the oldest surviving one in Jerusalem, many visitors and curiosity seekers began to stream there. The Karaites customarily purify themselves before entering the synagogue, so they do not allow guests. As the only Karaite on site, Rabbi Dabah found himself receiving the tourists and telling them about the community and its customs. With the aim of having the general public become familiar with the Karaite community, Dabah collected a number of its documents and objects and in the mid-1980s placed them as a small exhibit in a side room adjacent to the synagogue. In time, he managed to enrich the display with books and objects donated by the community, and in the early twenty-first century, he began to found a real museum. Two rooms adjacent to the synagogue were renovated, and the museum opened in its current format in about 2004 (Dabah, 28 May 2008; Bier, 1987, 118–19).

The entrance to the museum is concealed in a niche in the wall on Tiferet Israel Street, in a simple metal door with no sign or guidance.

On the walls of the museum's central space are plaques describing the history of the Karaites, their communities around the world, and the customs and traditions that distinguish them from most of the streams in Judaism, such as laws of *kashrut* (kosher foods), the placement of *tefillin* (phylacteries), and circumcision. The main exhibit in the museum is the reconstructed synagogue, which can only be partially seen through a large glass window. Next to it is a display cabinet, containing religious texts and ritual objects, most of which were brought to Israel by members of the Egyptian Karaite community, since the original objects used in the synagogue were plundered between 1948 and 1967. Presented in the next room is a wedding ceremony, and a few items of clothing, furniture, housewares as well as a small number of family trees and examples of traditional foods. Another room serves as a home for Karaite religious texts, but owing to their advanced age and high value they are usually not shown to the public.

FIGURE 26 | *Karaite wedding, display of the heritage of Children of the Bible (Karaite Judaism), Jerusalem, May 2008*

5.m. Turkish Jewry Heritage Center–Yehud

In 2002, Eyal Peretz founded the Arkadaş Association—the Turkish Community in Israel Association.[62] One of its goals at the time of the association's establishment was to create a museum for the history of Turkish Jewry. After Peretz received a building from the Yehud municipality, he renovated it and dedicated one of its rooms for a museum. The building and the museum located in it were inaugurated in June 2005 ("Opening for the General Public" 2005, 10).

FIGURE 27 | *Monument in memory of Ataturk, Turkish Jewry Heritage Center, Yehud, June 2006*

The objects in the museum were donated by association members, and Peretz arranged them as he saw fit, without any direction or professional guidance. The museum is developing slowly, according to the Peretz's time and energy as well as the objects he manages to obtain for the exhibit (Peretz, 20 Jun 2006). Displayed in the room is a mannequin praying in a synagogue and female mannequin in traditional costume in her home with a few housewares. One corner has a reconstruction of part of a wooden house, with a small kitchen, a sewing table, wall clock, and various housewares. Likewise, miniature models of houses in Istanbul are displayed.

FIGURE 28 | *Exhibit space, Turkish Jewry Heritage Center, Yehud, June 2006*

5.n. Bukharan Jewry's "Mini-Museum"—Kiryat Malachi

This is a small exhibit, "a mini-museum and library" as written (in Russian) on the entry door to the small, crowded room in which it is located, in a hut used as a synagogue for the Bukharan community. According to Michael Mordechayov, the representative of the Bukharan Jewry's Congress in the city, this is the first synagogue that was founded in Kiryat Malachi. The exhibition came about at the initiative of the elders of the local community, who were looking for a place of their own to display objects they had brought with them when they immigrated to Israel. Attempts began a few years ago to raise money toward establishing a real museum, thus far unsuccessfully. In May 2008, it was decided to concentrate the items temporarily in the synagogue. Many families of Bukharan origin have already expressed willingness to contribute additional items when a museum-worthy structure will be built (Mordechayov, 17 Aug 2008). As of now, the collection contains a small number of housewares and traditional garb, as well as pictures, community periodicals, and an assemblage of articles about the *edah* that have appeared over the years.

FIGURE 29 | *Traditional implements, Museum of Bukharan Jewry, Kiryat Malachi, August 2008*

5.0. The Bene Israel of India Heritage Museum—Beersheba (a Museum in Planning)

Reuven Raimond immigrated from India to Israel with his parents in 1970. He tells that when his grandchildren began to ask him about family history, he looked for written material about the Bene Israel community in India and discovered that there were neither books nor studies on the subject. When he located family members who had memories of life in India, he looked for a way to preserve and accumulate the information, and that is how the idea came to him to found a museum. He journeyed to India a number of times, collected documents and documented buildings that had been used by the community: synagogues, cemeteries, and schools. At the same time, he began to gather objects that had been used by the community, thus far mainly clothing and kitchen utensils (Raimond, 16 Aug 2007).

In 1996, Raimond, along with six friends, established the Razei Gahelet Association, with the aim of promoting the founding of the museum. The association produced a booklet with a comprehensive plan for setting up a center that would encompass a museum, research center, library, auditorium, cafeteria, and more. The plan, called "The Eighth Wonder," was presented to the Beersheba mayor Yaakov Turner, who expressed willingness to allot space in the city for realizing the plan.

In the meantime, Raimond and the other members of the association are dealing with fundraising and enlisting people to help, with the objects being stored for now in private homes. Since the association's founding, temporary exhibitions and displays have been held in community centers, schools, synagogues, and other public venues. Thus far, ten such exhibitions have been held in Beersheba and other cities in which live representatives of the Bene Israel community. Beside exhibitions, the association initiates studies on the history of the community, through academic institutions as well as the "Inexhaustible Springs" project for interviewing the elders of the community in Israel and in India and for documenting traditions that were handed down orally (Raimond, 16 Aug. 2007).

5.p. Museums in Various Stages of Planning

As we were conducting this study, a number of new ethnographic museums opened, while others are in different planning stages—from voicing the idea and initial fundraising to approval of plans and the start of construction. On the planned museum for the heritage of the Bnei Israel community of Indian origin, I chose to provide details above, since the association that initiated its establishment has already held exhibitions and carries out other activities, even though the museum has not yet been built. I have chosen, however, to not write extensively about other projects that have not yet been realized, if only because from experience I know that not all of them will reach fruition. For example, it was reported in the 1980s that in the planning stages were a museum for the Kurdish *edah* in Mevaseret Zion, a museum for the history of Russian Jewry in Jerusalem, museums for Indian heritage in Netanya and Haifa, a museum for the Samaritan community in Holon, and a museum in Ashdod for the various *edot* in the city (Inbar and Schiller, 1988, 18).

Despite that, I will mention a few other projects with which I have become familiar. For a number of years now the Bahalachin Association for the Heritage of Ethiopian Jewry has been working toward establishing a museum in Jerusalem. Many associations are working for the same goal at the same time, which perhaps is the reason for the foot-dragging preventing the founding of the museum. A law was even proposed in the Knesset and discussions were held on the issue but with no real progress being made. Occasionally, information appears in the media that a museum dedicated to Ethiopian Jewry is going to be built in one place or another, but thus far there is no museum (Knesset Committee for Immigration, 7 July 2008; "A Museum for Ethiopians," 2002; Sanbato, 2006, 14–20). Planned for Or Yehuda is a large center for the heritage of Bukharan Jewry. Likewise, in various stages of planning are museums for the heritage of Bulgarian, Romanian, Greek, Persian, and Dutch Jewry.[63]

Of late, the Knesset, too, has discussed in private bill proposals the establishment of new museums and heritage centers for different *edot* on behalf of the government. In 2000 alone more than 15 proposals were tendered to found heritage centers for Sephardic, Tunisian, Bukharan, Ethiopian, Libyan, Caucasian, and Georgian Jewry, as well for the Circassian and Druze communities.[64] Not all of these proposals explicitly included the establishment of a museum or an exhibit, but all of them dealt with the construction of a physical structure in which research, preservation, and commemoration activities for the heritage of the various communities would be carried out. Most of the proposals were presented by Knesset members of the relevant *edot,* and the majority of them were discussed in different Knesset committees, but were not brought forward even for a first reading in the plenum. Government representatives consistently opposed these proposals, mainly owing to budgetary reasons, but also for practical reasons that reveal the difficulties inherent in the intervention of the government in promoting heritage and commemoration.

For example, in 2000 Rahamim Malul of the Shas faction brought up for discussion the establishing of "a center for the commemoration of Sephardic Jewry: its rabbis and its poets," as a result of the founding by law of centers for the commemoration of Prime Ministers Rabin and Begin. In the discussion held about the proposed law in the Education and Culture Committee, the representative of the Legal Department of the Education Ministry expressed opposition to it and noted that her ministry does not consider it proper to interfere in this type of activity, which was liable to limit the communities themselves. She stated that "Each community wants to create its own activities, to commemorate and do research on it by itself ... there is a corporation that is Yad Ben-Zvi, and it is in charge of research, but we want to give the communities their own freedom and not to spend huge amounts."[65]

In the discussion on the proposal of a "law for the study of the heritage of Ethiopian Jewry," in 2001, the representative of the Ministry of Science, Culture, and Sport voiced a similar approach, to whit, the State prefers to support existing institutions that have been founded by members of the various communities over establishing other corporations by law. These, should they be established, would be bound to meet the criteria of statutory corporations, for example, that the members of their boards would be appointed by political ministers.[66] Moreover, representatives of existing institutions that attend discussions consistently came out against founding additional bodies, at a time when there are already were quite a few organizations dealing with the endeavor, some of which had been established by force of previous laws and were not receiving sufficient resources.[67]

Even so, in 2007, the Knesset did approve the establishment of three new heritage centers with state funding: the National Authority for Bukharan Jewry Heritage, the National Authority for Libyan Jewry Heritage, and the Center for Druze Heritage in Israel. According to the wording of the laws, only the last explicitly states that the heritage center will include a museum "for the maintenance of a collection of objects on the issue of Druze heritage and for a permanent exhibit of the collection or part of it" (Ministry of Justice 2007, 328). In the discussion held before bringing the bill to first reading in the Knesset, it was even stated that a previous government decision had already allotted a fitting site for the construction of the center in the area of the Yanuh-Jat local council in Upper Galilee.[68] If it will become reality, this will be the first museum in Israel devoted to a specific community established by a government decision and with the State of Israel's funding.

Chapter 6

᪽

Museums of Arab-Palestinian Communities

Just like the Arab-Palestinian national movement, Arab-Palestinian historiography also developed later relative to its Zionist parallel. One of the reasons is that the area called "Palestine" was first defined as an independent political entity only in the British Mandate period (Doumani, 1992, 9–10; Nassar, 2006). Identifying Arab "Palestinian" material culture, its definition, collecting it, and displaying it in museums all began in the British Mandate period (on that see above). This chapter deals both with museums located within the Green Line, as well as those in areas of the West Bank.[69] The connecting link between them is the opposition, even if passive, to the Zionist movement and the State of Israel, and the ideological connection to the Palestinian national movement.

The 1948 war disrupted the continuum of Palestinian existence, and as a result the Palestinian population was divided into three main groups: Palestinians citizens of Israel; Palestinians living in the West Bank and Gaza; and Palestinians in the diaspora, living mainly in refugee camps in Arab countries bordering Israel. Only at the end of the 1950s, and even more so in the 1960s, did Palestinian national consciousness reawaken, and in this period, Palestinian historical writing began anew (as did literature and poetry), in an attempt to document the Nakba (the displacement that preceded and followed the Israeli Declaration of Independence in 1948), and to understand it (Hammer 2005, 43). In this period various charity organizations began to form and operate in the refugee camps in an attempt to revive the art of embroidery, which was on the brink of extinction. Within this framework, workshops were established for young Palestinian women to study the traditional art of embroidery, and on the basis of them, a number of collections were assembled in museums in Jordan, Lebanon, and the West Bank (Kawar and Nasir, 1980). This is the background for the establishment of three of the museums described in this chapter, in Bethlehem, Jerusalem, and al-Bireh. In time, additional small museums and temporary exhibits on Palestinian ethnography were put together in Nablus, Bet Sahur, and Jericho as well as in Gaza. All were based on private collections and some of them no longer exist (Hamdan, 2001, 25–27).

The majority of historical museums in Israel take part in the structuring of the Land of Israel as the home of the Jewish people. As described above, despite the intentions of a number of museums to also present Palestinian content, they were never realized. The few that do, definitely stand out. One of them is the "Folklore of Minorities in Israel" an exhibition held in 1958 as part of the tenth anniversary celebration of the State of Israel. It was held in the Acre Municipal Museum at the initiative of the Minorities Department in the Ministry of the Interior, with the aim of advancing research and "mutual knowledge of residents of Israel who are members of different peoples." The exhibition included Arab, Druze, and Circassian objects and was divided into thematic sections: "Way of Life," "Manual Labor," "Man and His Garb," "Written Material," "Weapons for War and Hunting," "Household Implements and Crafts." One of the sections was called "Changes and Trends during the Decade of the State," in which were represented the "Changes and Achievements" of the minority groups as a result of the establishment of the State of Israel. The short descriptive catalogue was tri-lingual (Hebrew, Arabic, and English, in that order) (Lancet, 1958).

The establishment of the Palestinian Authority, in 1994, led to the first formal Palestinian activity in the field of preservation of heritage. As in the early years of Israel, the endeavor concentrated mainly on archeology, with the aim of proving the Palestinian people's right to the land.[70] This topic is organized by the Department of Palestinian Antiquities, which focuses on preserving buildings in the nuclei of historical cities. Part of these structures have been turned into museums, and in a portion of them are a few exhibits from the field of popular culture (Hamdan, 2001, 26–27).

At the end of the 1990s, the Palestinian Ministry of Culture began to deal with this area as well. One of the ministries' plans, never realized, was to establish a Palestinian memorial museum to commemorate the Nakba (see below). Another project, which was effected, was the documentation of items in existing museums and collections that are of cultural or historical value for the Palestinian people. The aims of the project were to protect the objects from theft, to encourage professionalization of the Palestinian museums' workers in the field of curatorship and preservation, as well as to create a data bank that would be of service to scholars. As part of the project, between 1997 and 1999, the collections of seven museums were systematically documented (Goldstein, 2003, 236–37).

6.a. Palestinian Heritage Center—Bethlehem

In 1947, a number of Bethlehem women established the Arab Women's Union, in order to provide immediate aid to refugees of the war with Israel. Its activity gradually expanded and during the 1960s, the Union began to preserve the embroidery tradition of the Bethlehem region. As part of this endeavor, in 1971 a museum was founded, in a historical building within the Old City (between Manger Square and Market

Square). The museum is devoted to the traditional material culture of the Bethlehem region, as it existed at the end of the nineteenth century and in the early twentieth. Two rooms offer a reconstruction of Bethlehem living quarters at the start of the twentieth century, including typical furniture. Another room is devoted to clothing and displayed in it are mannequins dressed in the unique, traditional clothing of the area of Bethlehem, and many embroidery works. Another room offers dozens of kitchen implements, storage vessels, and a small amount of traditional jewelry. In the early 1990s, another room was added to the museum depicting Bethlehem in the 1930s and furnished in the spirit of those times (Schiller, 1980, 50–53; Inbar and Schiller, 1995, 289; Kamal, 1998, 81).

6.b. Palestinian Folklore Center—Al-Bireh

In 1965, Samiha Halil, a politician and educator from Ramallah, founded the Society of Inash Al Usra (انعاش الاسرة; Revive the Family), which deals with empowering Palestinian women, and aid to Palestinian society in general. Among other activities, the society markets traditional embroidery works made by women in the area. In 1972, a Palestinian folklore center was established in the society's building in Al-Bireh that works for preservation of Palestinian culture, both tangible and the intangible. On site are a library and an archive and, from 1976, a small museum containing pottery vessels, traditional musical instruments, agricultural implements, a model of a Palestinian home and a restored reception room (Kawar, 1996, 9–10).[71]

6.c. Palestine Heritage Museum of Dar al-Tifel—Jerusalem

In 1948, Hind al-Husseini, a member of the Jerusalem Husseini family, happened upon a group of 55 orphaned boys and girls who had survived the Etzel and Lehi attack on the village of Deir Yassin. Al-Husseini, who had been a teacher and activist in women's organizations, decided to take the children under her protection and in the midst of war transferred them to Beit Husseini, the family mansion in the Sheikh Jarrah neighborhood (close to the American Colony Hotel). The building had been erected at the end of the nineteenth century by her grandfather, Salim Basha al-Husseini, who at that time was serving as the mayor of the Jerusalem municipality. Al-Husseini changed the name of the building to the "Arab Children's Home," and founded a school there, in which children from all over Palestine who had been orphaned in war studied. From then on, al-Husseini devoted her life to the education of orphans. She became well-known and popular among the Palestinian people (Stark, 2008, 19–20).

In the 1960s, al-Husseini also began her involvement with preservation of Palestinian material culture and bequeathing it to future generations, after becoming aware of its danger of extinction. She started to collect items by herself, and in 1969 she acquired a large collection of Palestinian folk clothing and housewares. The items had been amassed during the 1930s, by a group of Arab and British women with the aim of founding a national Palestinian folklore museum, a plan abandoned as a result of the 1948 war. In 1978, a cultural center and museum for Palestinian heritage was set up in the school. The school has expanded since then and now comprises a number of buildings. The museum is housed in the historical structure and contains some 3,000 items, including old furniture, embroidered dresses, jewelry, and various housewares made of pottery, glass, and copper. Beyond that, the museum displays traditional village life: baking of pita bread in a taboun, a woman carrying a water jug, and works by a stonemason and by a jeweler. The museum building also houses a library, a hall for lectures and performances, a crafts room, in which the school's pupils as well as those from elsewhere attend workshops to learn how to make things in traditional style. After al-Husseini's death in 1994, a room was added to the museum displaying her personal effects as well as objects she had made. At the end of the 1990s, the museum was closed to the public for renovations and renewal of the exhibit; it re-opened in 2012 (Dajani, 14 June 2008; Inbar and Schiller, 1995, 80–81).

6.d. Arab-Palestinian Museum of Heritage and Culture—Sakhnin

The collection of the items for this museum began in 1985, by the Research Center for Arab Heritage in Tayibeh. The museum was founded in 1990 by Adnan Farajallah. The display was situated in three dilapidated cellar rooms in an old building located in the historical heart of the city (then still a village), built in 1849 (Abu-Raya, 17 June 2006). The museum was established out of Farajallah's awareness of the importance of museums for reinforcing the national consciousness of Galilee Arabs, as one can learn from its goals, as they appear in its Hebrew publications:

1. Preservation of Arab heritage, with emphasis on its cultural and national character.

2. [The museum] is accessible to many scholars and students who are doing research on the topic of Arab heritage from its museum standpoint.

3. Proof of the Arab national identity and not obfuscating it in an attempt to reconstruct the history of the Arab-Palestinian person.

4. A learning tool for understanding the lives of the forefathers and the ancient heritage, as well as presenting the unique and shared elements among all

the Arabs, with an attempt to underscore the positive facets of Arab heritage and its contribution to the fashioning of the life of man socially and culturally.

5. Prevention of theft and imitation of the heritage—which is presented as it is, with no distortion.

6. Preventing commercialization of Arab culture—displaying the exhibits in a realistic manner—and the creation of a true imitative model of the heritage.[72]

In its early years, the museum mainly attracted the local Arab population, but within a few years, when it was publicized in Hebrew sources as well, it gained popularity among Jewish Israelis who appreciate ethnic tourism, particularly as part of organized tours.[73] This is how the museum, which began as a municipal institution to strengthen the national consciousness of the local inhabitants, gradually became an institution also addressing Jewish Israelis with the aim of challenging the preconceptions of the Jews who come to visit the city. According to Farajallah, the Jews are exposed to "authentic" Arab exhibits when they visit a museum on the history of settlement in one of the moshavim or kibbutzim. The Sakhnin museum constitutes an attempt to introduce into the consciousness of the Jewish public the fact that this is actually a part of Palestinian culture (Stein, 1998, 107).

The museum's current director is Amin Abu-Raya, of the "Knaan Association for Culture and Science." Abu-Raya is also the museum's only worker (as he puts it, "this is a two-hand museum") (Abu-Raya, 17 June 2006). Today, the museum occupies most of the building's area and comprises seven exhibition spaces devoted to various topics. Agricultural devices and implements are scattered in the courtyard, including a cistern and a taboun for outdoor baking.

FIGURE 30 | *Agricultural tools, Arab-Palestinian Museum of Heritage and Culture, Sakhnin, Feb. 2007*

FIGURE 31 | *The Diwan, Arab-Palestinian Museum of Heritage and Culture, Sakhnin, Feb. 2007*

Displayed in the room for tools are instruments that were used for various traditional crafts, such as carpentry, blacksmithing, and quarrying. Offered in the supply room are exhibits of different types of storage containers for agricultural produce (jars, baskets, jugs, and so on). Placed in the diwan (living room) are mannequins presenting typical figures of the traditional village: the village head (*mukhtar*), the religious leader (*imam*), the intellectual, the entertainer, the coffee server. In a room of the "family house" are female mannequins caring for infants and preparing food. The upper story is devoted to the varieties of Palestinian embroidery. Shown in the main room are embroidered dresses, each from a different region: Jenin, "the Triangle", Khan Yunis, Hebron, Ramallah, Jericho, Nazareth, Gaza, and Nablus. On the display tables are jewelry from different areas. The two adjacent rooms contain works of embroidery and other handicrafts.

FIGURE 32 | *Family home, Arab-Palestinian Museum of Heritage and Culture, Sakhnin, Feb. 2007*

6.e. The Museum of Palestinian Memory—Al-Bireh

At the end of the 1990s, the Palestinian Ministry of Culture began planning a museum of Palestinian memory. The project was led by members of the Culture Ministry, assisted by the Palestinian intellectual and academic Ibrahim Abu Lughud, as well as professional consultants for museum affairs from France. The museum has, to be sure, not yet been established, but the plans inform us of the importance that Palestinian society ascribes to museums as an instrument for constructing their national identity. The content of the planned exhibit focuses on the results of the 1948 war: the destruction of more than 400 Palestinian villages, turning their inhabitants into refugees. The destruction and loss of the homeland, an event that had already in 1948 been dubbed the "Nakba" (النكبة, "the tragedy" or "catastrophe"), has been a fundamental component of the Palestinian national identity and collective memory (Sa'di, 2002).

The original plan was to organize a network of museums in different cities in Palestine, with the first and main one destined to be founded in the village of Ein Siniya, north of Ramallah. Both the timing for the opening, as well as the planned location were symbolic: it was to open in 1998, the fiftieth anniversary of the Nakba, in the home of Abd al-Qadir al-Husayni, commander of the Arab forces in the Jerusalem region in the 1948 war, who was killed in the battle at Qastel and became a Palestinian national hero. The exhibit, too, was planned to focus on the symbolic and emotional level and not to be a historical, didactic one. It would include testimonies, pictures of destroyed villages, building stones from ruined villages, and the like. The main aim of the museum was to bequeath to the Palestinians a uniform historical narrative that could successfully compete with that of Israel. Thus, it was important to present not only the Nakba itself but also what preceded it and what occurred afterward. Within this framework, they sought to collect, preserve, and present collections of Palestinian ethnographic material that would attest not only to Palestinian memory but also to culture and history (Goldstein, 2002, 221–31).

Chapter 7

❧

Museums of the Druze, Bedouin, and Circassian Communities

Unlike the other museums presented in previous chapters, neither religion nor nationality, are the main common component of the museums in this chapter. The museums incorporated in this chapter were included in our study due to their similarity in form and not based on their content. In addition, we make no claim that there are similarities between the cultures and traditions of these ethnic groups. However, despite this, there is a possible resemblance among them regarding their political standing on the Israeli spectrum, and that similarity connects between the museums. An extensive discussion on this topic follows below.

7.a. Bedouin Heritage Center—Shibli

The village of Shibli, located at the foot of Mount Tabor, is populated by the remnants of the Arab a-Sabih Bedouin tribe, most of which scattered in Jordan during the 1948 war. In 1987, a Bedouin heritage week was held in the village; as part of it, an exhibit was held in which many Bedouin schools throughout Galilee participated. The local council continued to foster the site in which the exhibit was mounted. Afterward, the private collection of Diyab Shibli was added, and he was appointed director of the museum (Shibli studied museology at Tel Aviv University). Later, the council decided to close the exhibit, and Diyab Shibli chose to take it under his own responsibility. He moved the items to a building that he rented next to his home and reopened the museum in 2000 (Shibli, 1992, 72; Shibli, 17 June 2006).

FIGURE 33 | *Display hall, Bedouin Heritage Center, Shibli, June 2006*

FIGURE 34 | *Display hall, Bedouin Heritage Center, Shibli, June 2006*

At the museum entrance, a movie on the Galilee Bedouins is screened, and a few objects are hung on the walls. The exhibit is arranged in one large room, and contains traditional garb, housewares, vessels for making coffee, cooking and baking utensils, rugs embroidered in various stages of preparation, many agricultural implements, and personal items (jewelry, prayer beads, and the like). The exhibit does not have written explanations, and Shibli himself guides the visitors. Outside the building, there is a Bedouin hospitality tent, as well as a garden of herbs and medicinal plants, which in Shibli's opinion complete the exhibit. Shibli hopes to develop the place and complains that the local council has not made proper use of the village potential to attracts tourists, especially Christians visiting Mount Tabor.

7.b. The Sheikh Nasaradin Druze Heritage House— Daliyat al-Karmel

The museum was founded in 1995 by Amin Nasr al-Din in a souvenir store that he manages on the village's touristic Shuq Street. In charge of the museum today is Fadl, Amin's son, who had previously been a restaurant owner. As he says, the store has been owned by the family for many years, and many tourist groups who came to the area expressed interest in a place where they would be able to learn about Druze history and culture. The museum is located at the back of the store, in a room in which Yousef Nasaradin, chairman of the "Druze Zionist Movement" had lived. It is dedicated to him and his public activity. The museum mainly addresses groups of tourists, especially Israeli Jews. Druze do not come to visit the place, because, as he stated, "they learn about Druze heritage in school" (Nasaradin, 21 August 2007).

The Heritage House is named for Yousef Nasaradin, a business man and political activist who led the "Druze Zionist Movement," which he founded in 1975 in response to the UN General Assembly's "Zionism is racism" resolution. Over the years, Nasaradin promoted initiatives intended to turn the Druze community into a full partner in the State of Israel, and among other things, he started a joint project with the Jewish Agency called *Brit Hayim* (Covenant of Life; to distinguish it from the Blood Covenant that refers only to Druze service in the IDF) (Ashkenazi, 3 November 2005). The museum serves in an undeclared way as the voice of the family members' political opinions. Hanging side-by-side from the ceiling of the exhibition room is the flag of the Druze community and the flag of Israel. Plaques on the walls describe contacts between the Druze and the Jews before 1948; symbols of IDF units are displayed, and newspaper articles about Druze killed during army service and about the public activity of Yousef Nasaradin. There is no reference in the museum to friction between the Druze community and the State of Israel, against the backdrop of discrimination and inequality of rights, and there is no presentation of Druze who identify politically with Syria or with the Palestinians. More than just a museum, the location serves as a meeting place for Druze and Jews, who, as Fadl Nasaradin puts it, have "a thirst for amicable inter-community meetings" (Nasaradin, 21 August 2007).

The site contains very few original objects, mostly agricultural implements hanging on the wall and descending from the ceiling. The other "exhibits" consist of clippings of articles from the daily press, photos, drawings, and maps, which describe Druze life and their contribution to the IDF and the State of Israel. Visiting groups are offered food to eat there and to watch a traditional folklore performance or to take a tour in the old part of the village, guided by Fadl. To a certain extent, one may say that the Nasaradin family members themselves are the most authentic "objects" in the museum and, of course, the museum also serves to encourage tourists to enter and shop at the store.

FIGURE 35 | *Display hall, Druze Heritage House, Daliyat al-Karmel, Aug. 2007*

FIGURE 36 | *Historical documents, Druze Heritage House, Daliyat al-Karmel, Aug. 2007*

7.c. Circassian Museum (The Circassian Experience— The Museum for the Preservation and Dissemination of Circassian Heritage)—Rehaniya

The village of Rehaniya was established in the 1870s by Circassian refugees from the northern Caucasus who were exiled by Russia and were absorbed in the Ottoman Empire. To this day, most of the residents of the village are Circassians, with an Arab minority living alongside them. Shuki Hon, the museum's founder and director, became aware of the lack of Israeli awareness of their heritage when he served in the IDF as an officer in the Adjutant Corps, and people did not know what he was—"Iraqi or Persian." When he was released from the Army, he traveled to the Caucasus and happened to meet a man who was collecting ancient objects on the shore of the Black Sea; he then decided to devote his life to disseminating the Circassian heritage in Israel. When he returned there, he turned to the village council with that idea, but received no support because they thought this would not be economically viable. Hon decided to found the museum as a private institution and began to collect objects, mainly from his own family and friends. In 1997, the museum opened in the house in which he was born and where his parents lived, near the heart of the historical village (Hon, 30 January 2007).

Hon always serves as guide to visitors at the museum, while for the objects in the exhibits no explanation is provided. The museum is divided into three rooms. For visiting groups, a lecture is given in the entrance hall, along with a slide show. On the walls are pictures of the Caucasus, and there are mannequins of a man and a woman in traditional costume. One exhibition room is devoted to the home and presents a Circassian family in everyday clothing, household utensils, musical instruments, cooking vessels, and various appurtenances.

FIGURE 37 | Circassian *Museum, Rehaniya, Jan. 2007*

FIGURE 38 | *Courtyard of the Circassian Museum, Rehaniya, Jan. 2007*

The second room presents more festive clothing in display cabinets, a few weapons, and jewelry. Seen in the courtyards are agricultural implements used in the village in the nineteenth century. After concluding the visit in the museum, one may continue with Hon for a tour of the heart of the historical village, which passes through the location's gate and the mosque.

Hon says that he adapts his guidance to the type of audience and has learned over the years which stories "the Israelis love to hear" (Hon, 30 January 2007). With his guidance he provides anecdotes that stress the similarities between the Circassian and Jewish peoples, in the form of "just as the Jews say 'Next year in Jerusalem,' so the Circassians say 'Next month in the Caucasus,' or, 'For you the horn is a shofar, for us—a cup.'" During the stroll he stresses the close relations that developed between the Circassians and the Zionist pioneers in the early twentieth century and notes that the Circassians helped with the "illegal" immigration of Jews from Lebanon and that the obligation to serve in the IDF applies to them, too. He uses a large number of slang expressions taken from mainstream Israeli culture: *henun* (nerd), *dapa'ot* (IDF colloquial language: acronym for possible means of action), "the Polish mother-in-law" and so on. The exhibition itself emphasizes what is held in common and what is similar in the history of the two nations—their many years of suffering persecution and alienation in the original environment in which they lived.

This reveals the undeclared aim of the museum—to create sympathy among the Israelis for the Circassian minority living in Israel. As noted above, Hon established the museum as a result of the ignorance he encountered during his IDF service. In the museum, he tries to create among the visitors, most of whom are local Israeli Jewish tourists, identification with the Circassian heritage by stressing the letters displayed that were sent from dozens of Israeli groups that visited the museum, and particularly from many IDF units, attesting to the success of this goal. Notably, these components are entirely lacking at the other Circassian museum in Kafr Kama, whose founder and guide, Zuheir Thawcho, does not refer at all to the State of Israel or the Jewish people.

7.d. Samaritan Museum—Kiryat Luza

The Samaritans are a community whose religious faith is based on the Torah, who claim to be descendants of the tribes of Ephraim and Menashe, and who did not leave the country with the Assyrian exile. Samaritan tradition is based solely on the written Torah, so they assert that they are representatives of the "original Judaism," preserving to this day the customs of the Israelite nation as they had existed in the biblical period.[74] Today, the group numbers fewer than one thousand people, concentrated mainly in two neighborhoods—the Samaritan neighborhood in Holon and Kiryat Luza on Mount Gerizim (near Nablus), the mountain holy for the Jews according to Samaritan tradition. The group has been the focus of special interest among historians and scholars of religion, as well as among Christian pilgrims, especially because of figure in the New Testament parable of the Good Samaritan (Luke 10:25–37). Every year, the Samaritans conduct the ceremony of the Paschal sacrifice at a special site on Mount Gerizim, an event that attracts hundreds of scholars, tourists, and curiosity seekers.

Yefet Ben-Asher Hakohen (Husni al-Kahin in Arabic) belongs to the largest Samaritan priestly family and is likely to be appointed in the future as the high priest himself. In the 1980s, he realized that the many tourists and scholars coming to Mount Gerizim were quite interested in the Samaritan community, but there was no one to welcome them, nor any organized site they could go to in order to obtain information or ask questions. Thus he wished to create a museum. He felt that "creating it was imperative" (Kohen, 27 August 2008). In 1987, Yefet set up a small exhibit in his home in Nablus, but realized the location was not apt and that the Palestinians living in Nablus were not at all interested in the museum. In the 1990s, he moved to Kiryat Luza near the plaza where the Paschal ceremony is held and dedicated an entire floor of his home as a museum. After searching for financing for a number of years, Hakohen succeeded in opening the museum in 1997.[75]

In its first years, the museum was quite successful, and bus loads of tourists came to it. From the start of the Al-Aqsa intifada in 2000, there was a serious decline in the stream of visitors, but despite that, in 2008 Hakohen began to build a new structure, which will be separate from his living quarters and better able to provide services for tourists. As Hakohen sees it, the museum's ideological goal is to prove the Samaritan assertion that they are the remnants of the original Israelite nation. To that end, he musters his wide range of knowledge and feels that he succeeds in impressing and surprising those who come to the museum. In addition, the museum markets the *edah* throughout the world, and Hakohen says that many visitors come thanks to the Internet site.[76]

The museum is located in one large space, which has at its center a traditional Samaritan *sukkah* (with fruits as *sekhakh* [covering]) beneath which are chairs arranged for visitors. The chairs face the Torah ark that contains the community's Torah scroll. On each side of the ark are charts that present the history of the group, starting from Adam, and the lineage of the community's High Priests. Along the other walls stand display cabinets, containing models of Mount Gerizim and of the ceremony of the Paschal sacrifice, as well as various antiquities from archeological excavations done on the mountain.[77] Representing everyday life, mannequins are dressed in Sabbath garb; also seen is a home kit for preparing araq, a traditional craft widespread among the residents of Kiryat Luza.

FIGURE 39 | *Samaritan Sukkah, Samaritan Museum, Kiryat Luza, Aug. 2008*

FIGURE 40 | *Set for preparing araq, Samaritan Museum, Kiryat Luza, Aug. 2008*

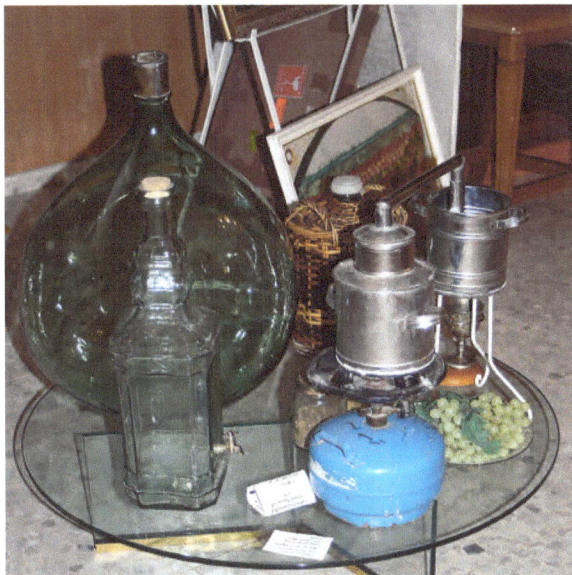

7.e. The Circassian Museum—Kafr Kama

Kafr Kama is a Circassian settlement in Lower Galilee, and like Rehaniya, was established in the 1870s by Circassian refugees, and most of its inhabitants are Circassian. Zuheir Thawcho, the founder, tells that each Circassian hopes to restore Circassian culture. Some do this through dancing, food, research, and in his case—establishing a museum. In 2001, he began gathering an orderly collection of objects, mainly from legacies of people who had intended to discard them. In 2006, he found a location, previously a restaurant, and began working on the museum, which opened in January 2007. He sees the aim of the museum as general support of the Caucasian homeland and improvement of the attitude of the residents of Israel toward the Circassian community, which for political reasons was "attached" in Israeli consciousness to the Druze community (Thawcho, 21 August 2007).

The museum is divided into two separate exhibition spaces referring to two different periods in the life of the Circassian nation. The first part is devoted to Circassian culture as it existed in the Caucasus and was brought from there by the founders of the village. It comprises three rooms, presenting items the Circassians brought with them from their point of origin: traditional clothing, a great deal of housewares, equipment for dealing with infants, traditional cooking implements, and the like. In the larger of the rooms, plastic chairs are arranged for visitors and there Thawcho tells the history of the Circassian people. The second part of the museum is devoted to the local material culture of the Circassians in Kfar Kama at the end of the nineteenth and in the early twentieth century. This is a relatively large hall containing mostly various agricultural implements, as well as tools kept outside the houses, and in his explanations Thawcho stresses that the tools are local ones that do not look like the ones common in the Caucasus.

FIGURE 41 | *Circassian Museum, Kafr Kama, Aug. 2007*

FIGURE 42 | *Circassian Museum, Kafr Kama, Aug. 2007*

Chapter 8

୶

Local Museums

In our search for ethnographic museums, many a time we came across museums exhibiting the history of the settlement or the region in which they are located. The aim was not to create municipal museums, that is, museums in whose founding or administration the local authorities were involved, such as the Tel Aviv Museum, the Nahariya Museum, the Beersheba Museum, and the like. We are also not referring to museums presenting certain historical events, such as Independence Hall, devoted to the establishment of the State of Israel; the Museum of the Fifth Aliyah in Kiryat Bialik; or a variety of museums displaying the history of Zionist settlement in Palestine. Alternately, the reference is to museums exhibiting the history and material culture of the settlement in which they are situated, in a general manner. Sometime, when local history is interwoven with the history of a certain community, or a limited number of them, a large part of the display is dedicated to presenting those groups. In those cases—there are three instances—we chose to include the museum in this study.

8.a. Joe Alon Center for Regional Studies, Lahav Forest

The museum began with archeological collections that accumulated in kibbutzim of the northern Negev and whose collectors sought a permanent host for exhibiting them. In the early 1970s, the findings were concentrated in kibbutz Lahav, and it was decided to found a regional museum there. The project was led by Uzi Halamish, who had previously served as head of the Benei Shimon Regional Council, within whose boundaries kibbutz Lahav is located, and he still serves as its general director. Its establishment was made possible by contributions from a number of government and private sources, mainly a donation from the Joe Alon Association.[78] Ongoing support also came from the Jewish National Fund. In 1973, construction began near the kibbutz; the museum was dedicated in a limited format in 1975. The exhibit's emphasis, as noted, was on display of archeological findings from the area, and alongside them, items that were collected by members of Lahav from among their Bedouin neighbors (Halamish, 16 Aug. 2007; Navon, (1988), 105–8).

FIGURE 43 | *Every-day objects in Sinai, Joe Alon Center, Lahav, June 2006*

In that period, a large private collection of objects representing Bedouin tribes of the Sinai Peninsula was created by Orna Goren, an Israeli who lived with her family in southern Sinai from 1975. Goren planned to establish a museum for Bedouin culture in 1980; however, as a result of the transfer of rule over Sinai from Israel to Egypt, the collection was moved to the Joe Alon Center, which was perceived as a worthy, authentic location. Supporting that was the fact that at that time there were no Bedouin tribes living in the region of Lahav forest, so claims of discrimination by one or another tribe were forestalled. Toward the consolidation of the collections, Halamish and Goren traveled to the United States and Mexico to gain impressions of museums devoted to native tribes. In 1985, the museum was reopened as a combination of the two collections, and since then, the Museum of Bedouin Culture has been the crowning glory of the Joe Alon Center (Navon 1988, 105–8).

FIGURE 44 | *Spinning yarn and weaving, Joe Alon Center, Lahav, June 2006*

Outside the museum building is an herb garden, including a section for herbal medicine, as well as a Bedouin tent, in which a visitor can hear stories and folktales, eat pita and drink tea. Despite all the attention devoted to Bedouin culture, it is important to Halamish to maintain the museum as an interdisciplinary study center about the place and its entire region, and not only for the field of Bedouin culture.[79] In line with that, other exhibitions have been mounted on site, such as a presentation on Jewish settlement in the Negev in modern times, the "Daroma" caves replica that contains examples of the caves typical to the area throughout history, and currently closed is the Bar Kochba Wing for the history of the Bar Kochba Revolt. A rooftop lookout atop the office building provides a wonderful view of the surroundings and even has a telescope for gazing at the stars.

FIGURE 45 | *The male host, Joe Alon Center, Lahav June 2006*

In contrast to most of the museums reviewed in this study, this one was not established by the community that constitutes the subject of the exhibit, that is, Bedouin society. Halamish takes care to point out that Bedouin representatives are on all the museum's committees, and the museum operates in full cooperation with the leaders of the tribes in the area. The museum guides are Bedouin from the 'Arab ar-Ramdin tribe, which prior to 1948 had lived in the region in which kibbutz Lahav is located today and now lives in the Southern Hebron mountains. Many Bedouin also visit the museum. In addition, in cooperation with the educators from the city of Rahat, a roving museum, "The Color of the Desert"—a mobile exhibit, which, by invitation, reaches Bedouin towns and villages, as well as Jewish schools throughout Israel—was created (Halamish, 16 Aug. 2007). Despite all the above, the museum has been criticized for not reflecting the many changes that have occurred in Bedouin society since the 1980s, the accelerated urbanization, and current social problems. The lack of connection to contemporary Bedouin society even led to the resignation of Orna Goren (Halamish, 16 Aug. 2007).

FIGURE 46 | *The woman in her home, Joe Alon Center, Lahav June 2006*

A new study by Havazelet Yahel, Noam Perry, and Ruth Kark aims to reflect multi-ethnic and multi-cultural societies within the Negev. This task placed it a priori in a challenging complex and controversial position, attempting to navigate between two different narratives. Yahel, Perry and Kark explore how the museum evolved through the years, presenting the different identities, and discuss its efforts to create a bridge between Jews and Bedouins within the Negev's polarized population. (Yahel and Kark, July 2016).

8.b. Beit Hameiri Museum—Safed

In Jewish tradition, Safed is considered one of the four holy cities, along with Jerusalem, Hebron, and Tiberias, and its Jewish community has existed there continuously since the Middle Ages. The first half of the sixteenth century is considered the "glorious era" or the "golden era" of Jewish settlement in the city. During the course of that century, Safed was the main spiritual focal point of the Jews in Palestine. Since then, its importance has declined, and with it the Jewish community has dwindled. At the beginning of the nineteenth century, the Jewish community began to grow as Ashkenazic Jews settled there, but in 1873 a severe earthquake destroyed large parts of the city (Amitsur, 2003).

Following this earthquake, the Hameiri family from Persia came to settle in Safed and established the Hameiri Dairy, "the first dairy in Eretz Israel," which is still in operation. In the 1950s, Yehezkel Hameiri, of the fifth generation since the family immigrated to Eretz Israel, began to inquire into the city's history. After finishing his army service, Hameiri began to work as a journalist for *Yediot Ahronot* and for Kol Yisrael, and he organized an office for himself in a large, ancient, empty, and neglected stone structure on the edge of the Jewish Quarter. As time passed, Hameiri bought and refurbished more rooms in the crumbling structure and filled them with old objects that he collected from people who intended to discard them, or by picking up items left on the city streets. At the same time, he met with the Jewish elders in Safed, from whom he collected certificates and documents. He interviewed them and documented their stories about life in the city from the end of the nineteenth century. For thirty years Hameiri worked on renovating the building and nurturing the collection of objects; he decided to establish in it a museum that would be devoted to the Jewish settlement in Safed in the past two hundred years, with the aim of "endearing Safed and its past to a wide audience." The museum opened in 1980 and was declared a recognized museum in 2000 (Mor, 2003, 195; 'Bet Hameiri', 1987, 11; Mor-Hameiri, 21 Nov. 2007).

**FIGURE 47 | *From the estates of the Elders of Safed,
Beit Hameiri Museum, Safed, Nov. 2007***

The exhibit in the museum was designed by Hameiri, according to his fields of interest and his own taste. The starting point of the exhibit and the guided tour is in the room devoted to the heroes of the museum—"Ziknei Safed" (the elders of Safed), the last scions of the families of the Old Yishuv, whom Hameiri interviewed and whose stories constitute the basis for the entire museum. Hanging in the room are their portraits, taken by Hameiri, which then underwent artistic processing; their life stories, and even some personal items, such as the canes used by some of them. The "Way of Life" room is devoted to daily life of the Jewish community in Safed, including, among other things, an original cistern that served the building's tenants. In the "Moments in Safed" corner are photos documenting figures and sites in the city in the 1950s and 1960s. "The Implements' Cellar" contains housewares typical of the times, and the corner devoted to "Plying Their Trades" describes the fields of employment and endeavor of the Jews of Safed. The "Safed Home" room reconstructs a typical scene in a Jewish home in the early twentieth century. "The Holiness of Safed" room houses a collection of ritual objects from private homes and synagogues, including important, rare items. In the room that served in the 1948 war as a front position of the Jewish Yishuv, the exhibition "Heroic Safed" has been mounted, dedicated to the topic of the security of the Yishuv from 1929 to 1948. The last room is devoted to the character and work of the museum founder, Yehezkel Hameiri, who died in 1989.

8.c. Treasures in the Wall— Ethnography Center of Acre and Galilee—Acre

Acre is one of the ancient settlements in Israel, which has been inhabited continuously for over 4,000 years. In the mid-eighteenth century, Acre became the most important city in Israel, when it served as the capital of Zahir al-Umar. Acre maintained this standing for about one hundred years, until the defeat of the Egyptian army and its retreat in 1840, during which the city was destroyed (Orman, 1983, 40–58). As an important port city and commercial center, which had survived throughout history, Acre became a limitless source for collectors of antiquities. One such is Dan Hortman, who amassed a large collection devoted to the urban culture of Galilee. At the end of the 1990s, he decided to found a museum, joining another collector, Michael Luria, to establish the Galileans Association.[80]

In 2005, the association received authorization from the Acre municipality to establish the museum in Burj al-Kommander (the Commander's Tower), a fortified compound built as part of the city wall in the nineteenth century by the then ruler of the city, Ahmad Pasha al-Jazzar. Dozens of institutions and private individuals were recruited to help with donations of other items, renovation of the structure, or advice. Overseeing the work of readying the museum was Shimon Mandler, a resident of Acre and collector in his own right, who today welcomes the visitors coming to the museum (Mandler, 27 July 2008). The museum opened in 2007, and according to the sign set in the entrance, it "illustrates and preserves the ways of life from the close to the end of the Ottoman era through to the early days of the State of Israel."

The museum is divided into two wings. The wing to the left of the entrance reconstructs a local marketplace, with various crafts and stalls: leather worker, shoemaker, basket weaver, hatmaker, goldsmith, potter, tinsmith, carpenter, clothes and textiles, apothecary, and others. The other wing displays various collections that were donated in their entirety: a reconstructed Damascene parlor, clocks, bells, keys, oil lamps, scales and weights, Armenian ceramics, matches, menorot

(Hanukkah lamps), Bezalel wood crafts, folk jewelry from around the Middle East, and much more.

Alongside some of the collections, a few details are provided about the collectors, but not about the objects themselves: where they were made, when, and by whom. Also, the museum places sole stress on the objects exhibited, but does not add information about the people who created or used them. Even though the museum states that this is an ethnographic museum, no reference is made to the ethnic identity of the collectors. Most of the objects displayed were acquired from non-Jewish residents of Galilee, but one cannot know that from the explanations on display. According to Mandler, the Arabs who live in the area scarcely visit the museum, since they do not have a culture of preserving the past the way the Jews do.[81]

FIGURE 48 | *A Damascene reception room, Treasures in the Wall, Acre, Aug. 2008*

Chapter 9

❧

Discussion:
Typology of Ethnographic Museums
in Israel

9.a. "National" Museums

The main theme of the five museums we have called "National," is their emphasis on the joint story of the Jewish people as a spiritual, cultural and, of course, national unit. To that end, they blur, intentionally, but also sometimes inadvertently, the differences between the ethnic groups with the aim of stressing what they have in common. Moreover, all of the founders of these museums were of Ashkenazi origin, from the elite of the Israeli hegemony. Despite their declared intention to glorify and promote non-East European ethnic groups, at times one finds in the exhibitions precisely Orientalistic concepts. This characteristic is particularly striking in the Israel Museum, in Jerusalem and the Eretz Israel Museum, in Tel Aviv. Both of them do have wondrously beautiful exhibits, based on extensive knowledge and in-depth study. Yet, in both of them, a structural division is discernible in the essential focus in the field of Mizrahi Jewish folklore (sparkling clothing, jewelry and so on), while in the realm of the "high" spiritual culture (Judaica and Holy Scriptures) greater expression is given to the Ashkenazic *edot*.

With that, one sees the continuation of the "melting pot" policy, which suppressed Middle Eastern culture, but ignored certain components that were considered harmless in the view of the establishment—the "low" culture, or the "folklore." The State of

Israel educational system, with its various branches, operated similarly elsewhere. For example, in the 1960s, along with the founding of "National" museums in Jerusalem and Tel Aviv, the Education Ministry consolidated a program for coping with the gaps in achievement between pupils from the Mizrahi groups, with those from Ashkenazic background. Towards raising the self-image of the Mizrahi pupils, elements from their source cultures were added to the curriculum. But the content did not include the history of Mizrahi Jewry, literary works, poetry, and so on, but rather, subjects taken solely from their folklore and popular culture. The topic that received the most significant representation was the festival customs of the various groups, and foremost among them—their holiday dishes (Horowitz, 1991, 13–14). Mizrahi food, as well as the magnificent jewelry, which was not worn every day, were perceived by the state institutions as elements that did not threaten the inchoate Israeli culture. Obviously, food and costume are fields identified with women, unlike politics, poetry, literature, and historical research, in which men usually dominated (Dahan-Kalev, 2001, 52).

To be sure, the large ethnographic museums occasionally hold comprehensive exhibitions about certain ethnic groups, and these displays not only garner great success, but also immeasurably enhance current knowledge, since they are accompanied by professional academic research and the publication of high quality catalogues. These, however, are temporary exhibits and they cannot serve as a substitute acceptable to each group's desire to have a place of its own that will constitute a permanent place of assembly and a source of pride to the group.

It almost goes without saying, yet it is imperative to do so, that in all the "National" museums there is no space for non-Jewish communities: Muslims, Christians, Bedouins, Druze, Circassians, Bahai, and others.

When the ethnographic wing of the Israel Museum began, it was intended to integrate within it exhibits of local Arab culture as well. The museum's warehouses contain relevant items, and some of them are even occasionally displayed for the public, but no comprehensive exhibit on this topic has ever been mounted and the exhibit today refers only to Jewish communities (Department of Ethnography, 1971; Muller-Lancet, 1974, 295). In Tel Aviv's Eretz Israel Museum there was an aim to set up a "minorities' pavilion" as well, but this plan too was never realized. The Ethnographic Museum in Haifa did display local, non-Jewish cultures found in its environment, but, as noted, this museum no longer exists (Benzur, 1985).

The anthropologist Kaylin Goldstein, who carried out an anthropological study on the Israel Museum, Beit Hatfutsot, and the Museum of the History of Jerusalem (the Citadel Museum), found that these institutions have great potential for creating intercultural encounters, which are likely to foster tolerance and openness to the Other. She even describes efforts by the museum directors, curators, and educationists working in them to promote an open, liberal policy, each in its own field. She claims that these attempts are a colossal failure since the professionals are locked into secular, Orientalist worldviews (Goldstein, 2003, 243–44). From the above survey of the other museums, apparently one may apply Goldstein's conclusions to all the "National" museums in Israel. Despite their declarations "on paper" that they are trying to cope with multiculturalism and to create a comparative dialogue among them, in actuality the large ethnographic museums fail to meet the task.

9.b. Museums of Jewish Communities

Despite the variety of museums representing the Jewish ethnic communities, one can discern many shared characteristics. First, one sees in these museums the conflict between loyalty to the Zionist movement, the feeling of belonging to the Jewish people, and the desire to remain separate and underscore the uniqueness of the group. The basic premise of the Zionist movement is that the place of all Jews—is Eretz Israel. Zionism considers the Jewish people one solid mass that dispersed and needs to be reunited in Eretz Israel. Upon the establishment of the State of Israel, tremendous effort was made to bring to Israel as many Jews as possible within a short period of time ("the ingathering of the exiles") and to turn them all into Israelis ("melting pot"). This process was accompanied by the diminishing of their other identity, the Diaspora one. The emotional process involved in that was well described by Amos Oz:

> The pioneering involved sacrifice and repression. People were forced to stifle "forbidden" yearnings for the landscapes of childhood, for the cultures of the nations among whom they lived, for treasured destinations, for a milder climate, for better manners, or large cities and their glory, and the parlor and the French language and the piano— all was silenced and suppressed with an iron fist, deleted from speech. Decades were effaced even from literature. Obliterated from the children's education. (Oz, 1979, 127)

Oz's statements refer to the Jews who immigrated to Palestine from eastern Europe before the establishment of the State of Israel, who voluntarily relinquished the mores of their previous culture and devoted themselves to ascetic pioneering. How much more so does this apply to immigrants coming to Israel after 1948, who had not chosen in advance to give up their culture. As for them, the policy of merging the Diasporas was expressed in what was dubbed "Negation of the Gola"—ascribing a negative value image to life outside of Israel, and all that pertains to customs, language, and garb. The identity of the "New Israeli" in his sovereign state was constructed entirely on the basis of negating the Diaspora-type culture (Raz-Krakotzkin, 1992, 23–24). Since the dominant culture of the State of Israel was built by Jews of European origin and in their image, the rupture was greater among Jews coming from Asian and African countries. Particularly in light of the fact that from 1948 on, most of their countries of origin were defined as "enemy countries," and accordingly the culture in which they had grown up and been educated were considered part of Arab culture (Shohat, 2001; Raz-Krakotzkin, 1994, 125–26). With this in mind, it is interesting that the two ethnographic museums expressing complete identification with the Zionist endeavor represent communities stemming from Arab-Muslim countries: the Babylonian Jewry Heritage Museum and the Museum of Libyan Jews.

The ethnographic museums of the Jewish *edot* in Israel are steeped in a complex conflict. They strive to glorify and present their culture at the height of its magnificence, but at the same time, this is a Diaspora culture, which the immigrant communities were required to abandon upon arrival in Israel. Demonstratively, all the museums representing Jewish communities identify totally with the State of Israel, with no wish to undermine Zionist values. They do this in a number of ways, with the most common being adoption of the supreme Zionist historical narrative. The typical demarcation of time for the museums of Jewish communities, which recurs in almost all of them, begins with the earliest historical attestations of the Jewish community in its location, continues with a description of community life in about the nineteenth century, and concludes with the group's *aliyah* to Israel, which is usually presented as an act of redemption. This choice, to cease the story with the immigration to Israel makes it possible to avoid confrontation with the Zionist narrative. In that way, the museums actually adopt the essence of the idea of the "melting pot," meaning that upon arrival in Israel the immigrants cease to be "Yemenites," "Iraqis," "Hungarians," or "Libyans," and become automatically "Israelis."

One may argue that the very presentation of Jewish life in the Diaspora as a primary element in their identity constitutes a challenge to the "classical" Jewish historical narrative. As part of negating the Diaspora, Zionist historiography drew a direct line from the biblical and Second Temple periods to the beginning of Zionism and the battle for the establishment of the State of Israel. In history books, especially textbooks, extra stress is placed on the three historical periods in which the Jewish people were "sovereign" in the Land of Israel, while in contrast the long period of the Diaspora is shunted to the margins of history, to the point of obliteration. The early Zionist historians wrote very little about the happenings of the Jews in the various places of dispersal but focused precisely on the lives of the few Jews who lived in the Land of Israel in this period, so as to stress continuous Jewish settlement in Israel.[82]

Therefore, completing the missing chapter can be perceived as undermining the Zionist narrative. Yet, most of the museums of the Jewish *edot* express their commitment to the values of Zionism by dedicating a great deal of space to Zionist activity among the community in the decades prior to immigration to Israel. Sometimes, as was done in the Babylonian Jewry Heritage Museum and in the Museum of Libyan Jews, there is over-emphasis, as if the Zionist endeavor served as the focal point in community life, while ignoring other voices. A portion of the museums, make pronounced use of Zionist symbols.

For example, in the Memorial Museum of Hungarian Speaking Jewry stress is placed on Herzl's being a native of Budapest, even though he only lived in Hungary during his childhood. The mythological picture on the balcony in Basel is prominently displayed on the museum's Internet site, and it is even printed on the museum brochures alongside the photograph of Hanna Senesh–another mythological heroine of Zionism (see fig. 16). The museum's annual conferences are held in honor of Herzl Day—the 20th of Tammuz.[83]

Another way to express dedication to the Zionist idea is by stressing the assimilation of the *edah* into the State of Israel. This is done, for example, by combining the museum display with commemoration of the community members who died in the wars of Israel. Even though this bears no connection to the community's life in the Diaspora, in many museums one can find a memorial corner within the museum or adjacent to it. A few of the museums of the Jewish ethnic groups refer to the integration of Jews in the Diaspora countries, including national identification with the nation state in which they lived. For example, proudly standing in the courtyard of the Turkish Jewry Heritage Center is a monument in memory of Mustafa Kamel Ataturk, founder of modern Turkish nationalism. (See fig. 27.) Similarly, noted with pride in a short film shown at the Memorial Museum of Hungarian Speaking Jewry is the high level of patriotism of Hungarian Jewry, which was expressed, for example, in their fighting in the service of their country in the Hungarian war of independence in 1848 and in World War I. Displayed in the museum are medals for bravery awarded to Jews in these wars. Despite this, most of the Jewish museums make no reference to the possibility of assimilating in the Diaspora, and the examples provided here are exceptions to the rule that attest to the general case.

In conjunction with that, another common characteristic of the museums for the Jewish *edot* is the presentation of the community as a minority that suffered various persecutions and threats in the Dispersal. This should be viewed against the backdrop of the Holocaust in the Jewish-Israeli discourse, as the ultimate standard to which are compared events of the moment and possible future dangers to the existence of the State of Israel. Holocaust awareness is capable of changing the relative status of groups and individuals in Israeli society, when "their prestige" is determined by "the experiences of the Holocaust that they underwent" (Jablonka, 2008, 102–103; Liebman, 1981). As a result, different groups and people understood that they could make political (and budgetary) gains by stressing their suffering in the Holocaust. Communities that survived the Holocaust founded ethnic organizations in commemoration of communities that had been destroyed. Conversely, groups that had not experienced the Holocaust directly sought ways to take part in the national memorialization experience in order to attain legitimacy (Liebman, 1981). These trends are also reflected in ethnographic museums.

The most striking in this aspect is the Memorial Museum of Hungarian Speaking Jewry, which centers almost entirely on the Holocaust. As stated above in the description of the museum, the idea to found it came into being after the Lustig couple realized that in Yad Vashem and Beit Hatfutsot insufficient space was given to the story of Hungarian Jewry.[84] This is the vacuum the museum was intended to fill, and this is its main function. Above all, it serves as a memorialization project for some twelve hundred communities that were demolished.[85] Of the three exhibition rooms, two are devoted to the destruction of Hungarian Jewry, and the exhibits in them describe their death, as well as life in the shadow of the Holocaust. Special emphasis is placed on "Valor and Rescue," for example, in the extensive description of the activities of the Zionist underground in Hungary during the war or the mythological story of the Palestine paratroops. This close linkage between the Holocaust and valor is reminiscent of the state memorialization of the Holocaust in Israel, at least in its guise until the 1970s.[86]

Beyond the display itself, the museum staff deals with research into the Hungarian speaking communities that were annihilated during the Holocaust with the aim of serving as a comprehensive source on this topic. Included among the museum's activities are the collecting and documenting of the experiences of the Jews of Hungary and its environs in labor camps, with the assistance and cooperation of the Claims Commission; a project for documenting old Jewish cemeteries in Hungary; an extensive library with tens of thousands of documents; holding a memorial ceremony in the museum's yard on Yom HaShoah (Holocaust and Heroism Remembrance Day); and maintaining a bulletin board with photos of unidentified people, with the hope that someone from among the museum visitors will be able to help in identifying them, in the nature of the "Search Bureau for Missing Relatives" (Shalev-Khalifa, 2006,12). The aim of the educational programs offered to schools and youth groups is "to make the students familiar with the rich heritage that was annihilated in the Holocaust and to relate the story of Hungarian-speaking Jewry during the Holocaust."[87] That being the case, through the complex of its activities, the museum operates as a kind of Hungarian adjunct to Yad Vashem.

In contrast to the Memorial Museum of Hungarian Speaking Jewry, most of the museums of the Jewish ethnic groups describe non-European communities, so they cannot present the Holocaust as making a defining impression on the life of community. Despite that, other instances of persecution are displayed, with special stress placed on the link between them and the decision to immigrate to Israel. For example, in the Babylonian (Iraqi) Jewry Heritage Museum a prime role is given to the events of the Farhud, written in the panel describing activity of the Zionist Hehalutz movement in Iraq is that one of its tasks was "to protect the Jews in times of trouble," and that this activity "engendered confidence among the Jews and intimidated the Arabs." Similarly, in the Museum of Libyan Jews there is a "Yizkor Pavilion," a memorial pavilion, in which the Holocaust of Libyan Jews in commemorated as well as the riots that took place in 1945, 1948, and 1967.[88]

Another example of this phenomenon can be seen in the Yemenite Jewish Heritage House in Rosh Haayin. The explanatory sign at the entrance begins with a description of the good life of the Yemenite Jews in the fifth and sixth centuries. After that comes the statement that "the appearance of Muhammed symbolizes a turning point exceptional in the history of the Jews of Yemen. From then on, during all their years of exile until their *aliyah* to Israel, they changed from people with independent, free standing into a persecuted, subjugated minority." After noting the difficulties under Muslim rule, the explanation returns to a positive note: "The political oppression and negation of human rights from the Jews did not break their lofty spirit and did not debase them." Finally, their *aliyah* to Israel is described: "The Jews of Yemen, who anticipated and wished for this day for many years, packed their belongings quickly, and left the only home they had known, which for them was temporary in any event, with only one goal awaiting them: "to immigrate to the Holy Land." One of the photos shows Yemenite Jews, members of a silversmithing family, plying their trade in a workshop in Bezalel in Jerusalem. Symbolically, this picture depicts the realization of the Zionist aim—the immigrants overcame the hardships and joined the circle of "Hebrew labor" in Israel.

These examples, which show the use of national oppression as a principle motif in the historical narrative presented in the museums of the Jewish *edot*, are embedded in a broader historiographic context. As described above, the Iraqi Jewish community fought for recognition by the state memorialization institutions in Israel to have the events of the Farhud considered part of the Holocaust. Similarly, the Libyan Jews struggled for recognition that they were victims of the Holocaust and for their inclusion among those receiving compensation as part of the Reparations Agreement. As for the Yemenite Jews, one can understand the museum exhibition as an echo of the debate among the historiographers of Yemenite Jewry, who over the years created two parallel, yet contradictory narratives. The first describes the Jews of Yemen as people who enjoyed a life of economic ease, as well as freedom of religion, and chose to immigrate to Israel simply for ideological reasons. According to this narrative, the Yemenite Jews are no less pioneering than the Jews who came from Europe. The second narrative depicts Yemenite Jewry as a persecuted community, which very frequently suffered from government decrees and needed the help of the Yishuv in Mandate Palestine. The historiography was fashioned according to the community's needs of the moment (Klorman, 2006).

In contrast to these museums, at the Cochin Jewish Heritage Center pride is taken in Cochin Jewry not having suffered at all from persecution in India, so their *aliyah* to Israel came from purely Zionist motives. These ideas are stressed in the guide given to the visitors to the center (Fenichel, 2005, 136). In addition, the Cochin community of Nevatim is presented as realizing Zionist values of "Going to the

Desert and taking root in the land through their own effort, without complaining about the establishment (Fenichel, 2005, 141). This is a negative example of the way in which the Jewish communities make use of the museums as a weapon for writing history, such that their story will fit into the Zionist-national super-narrative and become part of it.

Almost ironically, in the German-Speaking Jewry Heritage Museum, the presence of the Holocaust is barely discernible and receives minimal representation. This is not happenstance, but the result of the declared wish of the museum founder, Stef Wertheimer, to present German Jewry in its greatness, in its Golden Age, a story that he feels was forgotten owing to the Holocaust (Shiloni ,1998, 10). The main story that he chose to present in the museum is the extensive contribution of German Jewry to public life in Germany and afterward in Israel, in a variety of areas: culture, art, politics, commerce, science, and so on. After the museum was moved from its original location in Nahariya to its present home, as part of the Tefen Industrial Park, it was refurbished under the leadership of the curator Ruthie Ofek. One of the changes was the addition of a white wall upon which hangs a yellow badge upon which is written "Holocaust," dividing the section dealing with the Zionist movement in Germany and the one addressing integration into Mandate Palestine and the State of Israel, which ends the exhibition. Since the wall contains no items or explanations at all, it is clear that its presence is symbolic and rhetorical. The Holocaust is presented as something that, on the one hand, cannot be ignored, while on the other, there is no desire to treat it directly. This seems to be a compromise between the wishes of Shiloni, whose spirit is still palpable in the museum (he died in 1996), and Ofek's approach, who attests that she is very careful when making conceptual changes in the museum (Shiloni, 1998, 9).

Another striking characteristic in the museums of the Jewish *edot* is the central role given to religion, which is presented as a unifying factor that preserved the community in the Diaspora. The most common objects, found repeatedly in almost every museum, are those related to Jewish religious rites. These include items used by entire communities, such as ritual objects and furnishings from synagogues, Torah scrolls, and other religious works as well as religious objects used in families or by individuals: *tallitot* (prayer shawls), *kippot* (head coverings), tefillin (phylacteries), *mezuzot*, utensils and vessels for the Sabbath and holidays (candlesticks, Passover plates, Hanukkah *menorot*), and the like. Many museums have a reconstructed synagogue or a model of a synagogue, which in most cases is the most prominent exhibit in the museum—often the crowning glory of the display.

It was Shlomo Umberto Nahon who conceived and initiated the tradition of transferring Jewish synagogues from around the world to Israel, who in the 1950s moved a number of synagogues in their entirety from Italy to Israel. Two are now in the Israel Museum in Jerusalem and the Eretz Israel Museum in Tel Aviv, and another synagogue became over time the Italian Jewish Museum in Jerusalem (see above chapter 5). When the assembly of the Italian synagogue was completed at the Eretz Israel Museum in Tel Aviv, the director of the ethnographic pavilion, David Davidovitch, stated that the synagogue would actually serve the area's residents and the museum visitors (Davidovitch, 1976, 217). This hope was never realized. Only rarely does a museum synagogue attract a regular body of worshippers and conduct services. In the case of the synagogue in the Italian Jewish museum, for example, we know that the museum was instituted around the synagogue after thirty years.

Reconstructed in the Memorial Museum of Hungarian Speaking Jewry is the Torah ark of the synagogue in Tokaj, Hungary. The Lustig couple found the remains of the synagogue neglected during a visit there in the 1990s, and they managed to move the ark to Israel in 2000, where it was restored. A separate room of the museum was dedicated to the synagogue, and the exhibit includes both an explanation about it and the story of bringing it to Israel and its reconstruction. The museum even offers among its educational programs a workshop on "the rescue of the Torah Ark from Tokaj," which focuses on the restoration work.[89] Similarly, in the two museums devoted to Yemenite Jewry, the ritual objects are concentrated in one room, which represents a typical synagogue. In them, special emphasis is given to the figure of the *mori*, the rabbi with whom the boys studied Torah, who was the leading figure of the Yemenite community. Moshe Oved noted that for the founding of the museum in Rosh Haayin it was particularly important to him to emphasize the contribution that Yemenite Jewry can make to the Jewish world on the religious level, since in Yemen ancient customs and traditions were maintained that did not survive elsewhere (Fenichel, 2005, 110).

Another characteristic common to the museums of the Jewish *edot* is that their founders are usually politicians or local educators. They see the museum as an instrument for realizing their political or educational goals, both within and outside the community. The most outstanding example is the establishment of the Babylonian (Iraqi) Jewry Heritage Museum by Mordechai Ben-Porat. He wrote that "when I was a Knesset member I also served as the head of the Or Yehuda local council for fourteen years. In that period, we of the council decided to allot a piece of land for free to whoever would wish to erect a building for the preservation of their community's heritage. At that time, the population of Or Yehuda was a mosaic of new immigrants from different *edot*. The first to make use of this possibility were those stemming from Iraq"

(Ben-Porat, 1993, 34). Of course, it was not by chance that the Iraqi emigré community was the first to establish a museum in Or Yehuda, since Ben-Porat himself had been from the outset the one to think of the idea of founding it.

9.c. Museums of the Arab-Palestinian Communities

As with other Israeli cultural spheres, the Arab-Palestinian population is absent from Jewish Israeli museums (Hamdan 2001, 35). To be sure, Palestinian material culture is presented at times in "Jewish" museums, but not the Palestinians themselves. Their vessels and objects are not labeled as "Palestinian," or even as "Arab." This is the case, for example, in the Eretz Israel Museum, in the Man and His Work Center, which displays a variety of craftsmen working with traditional methods and tools: a smith, a harness maker, a blacksmith, cotton-carder, and so on. They are presented as local artisans, with no mention of the fact that most of the people plying these trades were actually Palestinians. Similarly, in the "Treasures in the Wall" Museum in Acre, thousands of items are exhibited, most of which were acquired from Galilee Arabs. The exhibit explanations, also given in Arabic, do not refer at all to the origin of the items but rather are presented as objects of "bygone days." The museum scarcely has Arab visitors, and the assumption of the director, Shimon Mandler, is that this stems from their "lack of interest in the past and history" (Mandler, 27 July 2008).

With this in mind, the main common characteristic of the Palestinian museums is the motivation to establish them, that is, the attempt to save the Palestinian material heritage and culture in light of its intentional eradication by the State of Israel. The most outstanding ethnographic exhibit among them is Palestinian embroidery, renowned in the Arab world for its high quality. The magnificent embroidered Palestinian dresses were exhibited as early as the mid-nineteenth century in the largest and most important ethnographic museums in the world. Especially engaging to ethnographers is the fact that for each geographic area there are embroidery patterns characteristic to it (Kawar and Nasir, 1990). All the museums in this category have an extensive exhibition of embroidery works, usually displaying them according to their geographic origin. The geographic distribution of Palestinian embroidery verifies, as it were, the structuring of the land as a single geographic unit belonging to the Palestinian people.

Another very striking characteristic in Palestinian museums is the link to agriculture. Presented in each of the museums in this category are traditional agricultural implements, such as the plow, the olive press, and the like. These exhibits underscore the historical connection of the Palestinians to the soil and the land. Moreover, the display of traditional agricultural tools provides a response to their appropriation by museums devoted to Jewish pioneering in Palestine. As Tamar Katriel argues concerning museums of Zionist settlement:

A large part of the displays in the subject called traditional agriculture are objects that an ethnographer of your type would ascribe in fact to some Arab village in a not so late period. Yet, often, the story of the objects appears as a biblical one … I spoke with Arab visitors who said, "Actually, this is our museum." But I spoke with Jews who said, "These are the tools of father and grandfather, and the stories belong to Moshe and Haim" (Katriel, 1992, 38).[90]

The Museum of Arab-Palestinian Heritage and Culture in Sahnin refers to this issue in its publications, by defining part of the aims of the museum as "proving the national Arab identity and not blurring it" as well as "preventing theft and imitation of the heritage," without noting who is the thief and the imitator. This is actually the only museum operating actively to reinforce Palestinian national identity, but by stressing the link to the land all the Palestinian museums are expressing rebellion, even if muted, against the Zionist narrative of "redeeming the land." For if the agricultural implements were in use even prior to Zionist settlement, then someone was working the soil, and the country was not "empty."

In contrast to the museums of the Jewish communities, the Palestinian museums do not contain any reference to religious components of culture, neither to Islam nor to Christianity. There are no reconstructions or findings from mosques and almost no displays of appurtenances of prayer or rites. In addition, while the Jewish museums stress the Jewish historical narrative of Diaspora life and *aliyah* to Israel, the Palestinian museums do not exhibit any historical narrative at all. Even concepts that have become basic notions in understanding the Israeli-Palestinian conflict, such as the Nakba or the refugee experience, are not represented in these museums. This is in complete contrast to the Jewish museums in which extensive space is given to the persecution of the Jews in the Diaspora.

9.d. Museums of the Druze, Bedouin, and Circassian Communities

Categorizing these museums on the basis of characteristics of their content is difficult. The Bedouin community in the Negev differs from that in Galilee, and both are distinguished from the Druze community and from the Circassian one. Theoretically, one could make a similar statement about the communities of Jewish origin as well, for example, Bukharan Jewry versus German Jewry. The main difference among the development of the Bedouin, Druze, and Circassian communities, however, is that there is not and was not a common national-historical narrative binding them together as the joint Zionist narrative does for the Jewish communities. If there is one thing that does unify them politically, it is that the attitude addressed and still directed toward these groups in the State of Israel, which—despite continuously growing protests—defines them as "minorities" and lumps them together with the Palestinian population so as to differentiate them from the Jewish population.

Despite the differences in content, there is a formal similarity among these communities that justified categorizing them together under a joint rubric. The most salient common characteristic is the dominant commercial-tourist aspect, which serves as the main component in the reason for their establishment, their appearance, and their administration. In that they are akin, even if not declaredly so, to the model of the commercial-tourist museum of the ecomuseum type, discussed above (chapter 2.3). The most prominent example of this is the store adjacent to the museum in which one can buy locally made products, mainly foodstuffs and clothing. The entry to the Druze Heritage House in Daliyat al-Carmel is through the store owned by that family. Yet, the store alongside the museum is a characteristic one can find in most of the museums, which find it difficult to locate sources of income. It is only for the museums in this chapter, however, that a restaurant is also included.

In contrast to museums in all other categories, the five museums discussed in this chapter are definitely geared toward making a profit. They are located at the center of tourist sites and were established by their founders, members of the community, with the idea that they could earn a living from operating them for the many tourists, who in any event, come to visit the places in which they are situated. At times, the initiators also noted educational or informational goals as additional motives, but it is clear that these were secondary to the economic incentive. That being the case, most of these museums do not meet the professional standards required of an official museum, and they are not even interested in receiving such recognition.[91] One must keep in mind, however, that this does not attest to the professionalism of the exhibition, which in some cases is quite meticulous and no less professional than in the official museums. It must be said, however, that on the whole one can see there is less precision regarding historical accuracy, an orderly registration of objects, proper storage conditions, and so on. In almost all of them, the collection of exhibits is relatively small and striking in their lack of historical exhibits.

9.e. Local Museums

The three museums covered in the Local Museums chapter, namely, the Joe Alon Center, Beit Hameiri, and Treasures in the Wall, are unique in two main facets. First, the most superficial, they are not "single-ethnic-community," that is, they do not present only a single *edah* or ethnic group. Rather they are devoted to the geographical space surrounding them, meaning they are museums of place. This is somewhat similar to other museums not included in this study, such as Yigal Alon "Man in Galilee" Museum at Ginossar, or even the visitors' center at Mizpeh Ramon. These two examples also refer to museums presenting their geographical environment, although the emphasis in them is on the physical environment and not necessarily the human. So these museums fit into the Zionist concept, originating in Germany, glorifying Land of Israel studies as a scientific discipline.

The second, and main, difference is that two of the museums were founded by people who are not members of the communities they present. The Joe Alon Center and the Treasures in Wall museum are devoted to the Bedouin community and to Galilee Arabs, respectively, but both were established by Jews and not by community members. As for Beit Hameiri, which is dedicated to the Old Yishuv in Safed, the family of Yehezkel Hameiri, the founder of the museum, immigrated to Safed in 1837 and was not part of the continuum of the *yishuv* (settlement) that is called the Old Yishuv. Thus, these three museums are more similar to the original model of an ethnographic museum, which was created by white people of European origin who presented "exotic" communities from around the world.

Chapter 10

❧

Conclusions

As part of this study, the field of ethnographic museums in Israel was mapped and five types of museums with distinct characteristics were identified: "National" museums; single-ethnic-group museums of Jewish communities; museums of Palestinian communities; museums of the Druze, Bedouin, and Circassian communities; and "local" museums not devoted any specific ethnic group. The "National" museums are recognized by the State of Israel; they are large and well financed. As for content, they represent the "melting pot" concept of the Zionist movement, which strives to unify the Jewish people into a single collective distinguished from its surroundings. From the point of view of the various communities composing the mosaic of the Israeli population, the greatest shortcoming of these museums is that they do not allot a permanent platform for each *edah* to stress its uniqueness. Actually, they are working toward an opposite goal—to emphasize what is similar among the communities and to repress what is different. Obviously, they also shunt to the sidelines, or totally ignore, the fact that large parts of the Israeli population are not Jewish at all.

In recent decades these drawbacks have been remedied by single-ethnic-group, or ethnocentric, museums that present communities with a single, common ethnic origin (Kark and Perry, 2008). Katriel explains that they offer "a picture of Jewish communities in the past, in all their glory." In other words, they present a specific culture as it existed elsewhere (ethnography) and in a different time (history), so they constitute an ex-categorical combination of an ethnographic museum with a historical museum (Katriel, 1992). Actually, the mixture of categories is even greater, since these museums, in many instances, also display art objects, Judaica objects, and even archival documents, which in accepted practice would find their place in other institutions (Yair, 2004, 90).

Mixing categories also created problems with terminology. Tamar Katriel calls them "museums of Jewish ethnography," a definition that includes only institutions of the Jewish *edot* (Katriel, 1992). Mordechai Ben-Porat dubs them "ethnic historical museums" (Ben-Porat, 1993, 15). The journal *Be-Muze'on* uses the terms "community museums" or "museums of the *edot*" (Editorial, 1993, 1). In a summary written by Lifschitz and Schiller, they make a distinction between museums of the Arab, Bedouin, and Druze, which they call "ethnographic museums," and museums of Jewish communities, which are called "museums of *edot*" (Lifschitz and Schiller, 1995, 270). Another terminological issue derives from the difficulty, or lack of interest, of some of these institutions in gaining recognition from the Education Ministry as official museums.[92] A few of them are large and impressive, but most are relatively small and suffer from severe financial constraints. Sometimes an entire museum is maintained by a "staff" of one or two people, "fanatic devotees," as Inbar calls them (Kol-Inbar, 1992, 25). Though some are called museums—even if they are not officially recognized—the majority are purposely termed "heritage center" or "heritage house." Whatever the name may be, the nature of the museum is determined mainly by the nature of the ethnic group it represents.

The single-*edah* Jewish museums began to develop in the 1970s at the same time as the counter movement that saw in the "melting pot" policy a tool wielded by the Ashkenazic elite to erase and blur the past of the Jews from the East and the Islamic countries. Among such museums are those, which describe the life of a consolidated, delimited Jewish community, such as, for example, the Cochin Jewish Heritage Center, which deals with communities that lived in southwestern India in the city of Cochin and its environs. In contrast, a portion of the museums encompass a Jewish culture that existed in a geographic area crossing political borders. This applies to the Worldwide North Africa Jewish Heritage Center and to the museums for the heritage of German- and Hungarian-speaking Jewry. In the middle are those that define themselves according to the modern, accepted borders today: Italy, Yemen, Libya, Iraq (Babylonia), Turkey, and so on.

The presence of the Holocaust in these museums is striking, and not without reason. The Holocaust constitutes a central component of museums in Israel. Most prominent among them is the Yad Vashem Museum, the State of Israel museum for the commemoration for the Holocaust of the Jews of Europe, which is the only museum in Israel established by the authority of a Knesset law and which is an "obligatory stop" for school students, IDF soldiers, and official guests of the State of Israel (Rousso, 2004, 4). Many other museums deal exclusively with the Holocaust, and beyond that there are hundreds of commemoration sites and monuments of communities and various organizations, scattered throughout Israel (Brog, 2005, 175).[93] Despite the plethora of sites for Holocaust memorialization in designated museums, the Jewish ethnographic museums also give the Holocaust a central place. This is so even in museums of non-European Jewry. The second motif prominent in the displays of the single-community Jewish museums, which is repeated in almost all of them, is their emphasis on the integration of the *edah* into the State of Israel and its contribution to Israeli society. The museums thereby relinquish part of the subversion accompanying the segregation of the group from the "whole Jewish people" and declare that they are essentially adopting the Zionist vision of unifying the different parts of the nation in Israel.

The Arab-Palestinian museums are more varied. Some are the direct successors of the more veteran museums in Israel, including those that were founded prior to the establishment of the State of Israel. Some are within the boundaries of the Green Line, while others are in the areas of the Palestinian Authority. The linking motif among them is the aspiration to preserve Palestinian heritage. While the heritage of the Jewish *edot* was effaced through "natural" modernization processes, Palestinian society in Israel in recent decades has been left with no political self-definition and is in danger of actual extinction of its spiritual and cultural heritage. One must add to this the cultural appropriation of traditional Arab agriculture by the museums of Jewish settlement in Israel (see chapter 6 for extensive discussion of this). In light of the foregoing, it is especially interesting that most of the Arab-Palestinian museums do not refer directly to this political reality.[94] They do not note the many wars, the Nakba, or even how daily life has changed as a result of these events.

The museums of the Druze, Bedouin, and Circassian communities were established mainly out of commercial-tourist motives. Even though a segment of these ethnic groups definitely identifies with the Palestinian population, and not with the Jewish population, the founders of these museums purposely refrain from creating this connection. Leading this trend are the Museum of Circassian Heritage in Rehaniya and the Druze Heritage House in Daliyat al-Karmel, both of which strive to bring their community closer to the State of Israel and its Jewish citizens.[95] Undoubtedly, alongside the ideological motivation stands the economic consideration, since most of the visitors to both museums are local Jewish tourists.

Beyond the nature of the community, which dictates certain content to the museum, the character of the museum is dictated by the nature, ambitions, and personal past of its founders. A museum is a complex institution, which requires experts in several fields: administration, curatorship, preservation, design, marketing, education, gathering resources, and more. Yet the greater part of the museums discussed in this study operate with a very small staff, often consisting of only one person, who collects what other people discard and devotes most of his energy and time (and now and then, his own money) to fostering the collection. This romantic figure, in Israel has been denoted by the phrase "fanatic devotees"—which has already entered the pantheon of Israeli clichés and has even been the object of critical culture analyses.[96] All of the museums described were established in this manner, without professional guidance. The "fanatic devotees," gradually succeeded in spreading their dedication to the venture to others. In some of the museums the "fanatic" becomes part of the exhibit through the guidance he gives.[97]

The character of each museum derives from the nature of its founder. So, for example, the Museum of Libyan Jewry would not have included such extensive reference to the integration of the community members in the defense forces were it not for the past of its founder, Avi Pedazur, in the Air Force. The Museum of Italian Jewry puts special emphasis on Italian synagogues as a result of the efforts of S. U. Nahon in bringing synagogues to Israel. The Babylonian (Iraqi) Jewry Heritage Museum was established precisely in Or Yehuda since its founder, Mordechai Ben-Porat, had previously served as the city's mayor. The fact of its being the largest and most impressive single-*edah* museum can be ascribed to Ben-Porat's fundraising abilities. Prominent by their presence among the group of people who established ethnographic museums are educators and politicians. Few of them had professional training concerning museums before founding one.

Yet, the ethnographic museum, like any museum, is essentially a political institution (Noriega, 1999; Azoulay, 1999, 76–77). One cannot ignore the fact that the founders are the ones who determine not only the nature of their museums, but also the historical narrative presented in it. For example, the two museums of the Circassian community paint very different pictures. The objects exhibited are very similar, but each museum chooses to accentuate a different narrative. Shuki Hon's museum in Rehaniya goes to extremes to stress the similarity between the Circassians and the Jews and the Circassian contribution in IDF service. In contrast, Zuheir Thawcho's museum in Kafr Kama emphasizes precisely the independent national identity of the Circassians and the link between the Circassians living in Israel and their place of origin. Despite the close relations between the communities in the two villages, Hon and Thawcho are not in contact and have not even visited each other's museums (Hon, 30 Jan. 2007; Thawcho, 21 Aug. 2007).

Beyond that, establishing a private museum also allows the founder to decide to ignore certain chapters from the life of the *edah*, or a certain population group. Even though most ethnographic museums deal with one given community, it is important to remember that it never involves uniform, monolithic communities. Thus, for example, the Memorial Museum of Hungarian Speaking Jewry presents almost exclusively middle-class people. Lacking are two other prominent groups—the Jewish families who were the giants of industry and finance, and Orthodox Jewry. As these two groups did not donate objects, so in line with the policy of the museum founders, they are not represented, as the entire collection is based on donations (Porat, 2006, 15–16).

Similarly, the Museum of Libyan Jewry mainly represents the urban community of Tripoli, and not others such as the Jews of Cyrenaica or the community of cave-dwelling Jews.[98] The Worldwide North Africa Jewish Heritage Center presents almost exclusively Moroccan Jewry, while those of Algiers and Tunis are marginally represented (also almost all donations came from Moroccan Jews).

Finally, there are common characteristics among ethnographic museums in Israel in the way they relate to the community to which they belong. These museums are nurtured by the communities that founded them, and the museums nurture these communities, in varied ways, in return. The "devoted fanatic," the community member who works assiduously to establish the museum, creates these links even before its founding, mainly for the purpose of fundraising and collecting objects and stories, resources without which his vision cannot be realized. A few museums really are one-man operations, but most are established through cooperation between people of vision and action and people of means. In many museums the names of donors are listed next to the objects they have given, and thus their memory is perpetuated. In the Old Yishuv Court Museum members of veteran Jerusalem families were invited to set up a family memorialization corner in which the family business would be presented.

The museum location may be of supreme importance to its ability to maintain ongoing connections with the community, and in many instances the site definitely influences the nature of the museum. Naturally, most ethnic museums were established in the places with a concentration of group members and developed over the years as focal points of identity for the community. For example, the Museum for Yemenite Jewry Heritage grew logically out of the high school in Rosh Haayin, almost all of whose students and teachers were of

Yemenite origin. The city of Or Yehuda was established on the basis of five temporary transit camps populated mainly by immigrants from Iraq, so there was no more obvious place for founding the Babylonian (Iraqi) Jewry Heritage Museum. The Internet site of the Turkish Jewry Heritage Center in Yehud notes that the center was established there "since Yehud absorbed many immigrants from Turkey in the 1940s and 1950s, and in terms of percentage, it is has the highest number of olim from Turkey."[99]

Other *edot* and communities are scattered throughout Israel, with no focal point serving as a "natural" site for setting up a museum. In such cases, the museum is most often established in a large city in the center of Israel, in the hope that it will be accessible to as large an audience as possible and will succeed in attracting many visitors. For example, the Museum for Yemenite Jewry Heritage of the Association for Society and Culture was erected in Netanya simply because this is where its founder, Ovadiah Ben-Shalom, lived and was active. Since Netanya is not a significant focal point for Yemenite immigrants and their descendants, the association created branches throughout Israel with the aim of forging direct connections with them. These branches were opened, for instance, in Jerusalem, Ashkelon, Kiryat Tiv'on, Rehovot, Misgav, Yakhini, Amka, and in the Mateh Yehuda Regional Council (Mizrahi, 2000, 24).[100] Similarly, the Memorial Museum of Hungarian Speaking Jewry, located in Safed, conducts activities for the "next generation" in the center of Israel so as to enable as many people as possible to take part in them.[101]

Sometimes the location is determined by practical considerations of its founders. For example, the Museum for the Heritage of the Jewish *Edot* was established in Lod since the city was historically a spiritual center of Torah learning, and because of its role in absorbing new immigrants. "The varied structure of the new population created a lively, active society, the full blending of the Diasporas of the east alongside the west, with each *edah* preserving its heritage and its unique character" (Saraf, 1979, 17). The museum enjoys the cooperation of the *edot* it presents, and the communities have easy access to the museum.[102] Similarly, the director of the Razei Gahelet Association, Reuven Raimond, who plans to establish a museum for the heritage of the "Bene Israel" community from India, insists that it be erected in Beersheba, since most of the community lives in the southern part of Israel and so that the museum will be able to maintain permanent contact with Ben-Gurion University (Raimon, 16 Aug 2007).

After the museum opens, it begins to give back to the community, and the circle of its influence becomes wider and wider. Aside from their existence as natural meeting places for community members, many museums serve in different ways to reinforce the connection with the community. For instance, many museums conduct periodic activities for the community members and their families. Sometimes, these events are part of the content that the museum strives to promote, such as conferences and seminars, cultural evenings, and memorial gatherings. In other cases, the idea is simply an attempt to create joint activities for the community members, such as days with an enjoyable program, performances, and trips. Many museums publish a newsletter distributed among the community with information on museum activities,[103] or they manage a website for similar purposes.[104] At times, the museum provides a source of livelihood for the community, especially museums and heritage centers of a touristic nature. For example, at the Bedouin Heritage Center in Shibli, alongside the exhibit room is a gallery of traditional handmade items made by the women of the village, and these can be purchased. Diyab Shibli, the museum's director, sees great importance in this museum activity and hopes that through it he will improve the earning ability of the women living in the village (Shibli, 17 June 2006).

Sometimes the museum serves as a bridge between the community living in Israel and the one in the country of origin. For example, a few museums conduct courses for learning the language of the country of origin or arrange "Roots" journeys to the community's previous home. The Turkish Jewry Heritage Center has set one of its goals as strengthening the links between the community of Jews in Turkey and fostering friendship between the Israeli and Turkish peoples.[105] The Museum of Italian Jewry holds events for the general public on Italian culture, and not only that of the Jews of Italy, such as an annual festival of art and pasta, as well as concerts of classical Italian music (Gafni, 28 Aug 2007). Coming to the Circassian Museum in Kafr Kama are residents of the village with their family members who pay visits from different places in the world (Thawcho, 21 August 2007). The Worldwide North Africa Jewish Heritage Center was founded by fundraising among the wealthy members of the community outside of Israel, and owing to the importance of the connections to them it was decided to call it a "worldwide" center (Gozlan, 31 Jan. 2007). For a similar purpose, the Museum for Yemenite Jewry Heritage in Netanya opened branches in the United States, Britain, Germany, Norway, Sweden, and the Netherlands (Mizrahi, 2000, 24).[106]

A link to the community of origin is also expressed in the languages used in the museum. In the room of Indian Jewry in the Museum for the Heritage of the Jewish *Edot* the captions on the exhibits are tri-lingual: Hebrew, English, and Marathi.[107] In the mini-museum of Bukharan Jewry in Kiryat Malachi, the captions are only in Russian. In the Arabic-Palestinian Heritage and Culture Museum in Sakhnin, the captions hanging on the walls are only in Arabic. The founder of the museum explained that, from his point of view, this is an intentional political statement, and that if the Israel Museum in Jerusalem does not have explanations in Arabic, there is no reason his museum should have them in Hebrew.[108] Despite that, for publicity purposes the signs at the museum entrance do have lines in English and Hebrew; moreover, the advertising brochures of the museum are produced in three languages. In the Arab Children's Home in Jerusalem (Palestine Heritage Museum of Dar al-Tifel), the explanatory notes for the exhibits are in Arabic and English. Information about the museum is published only in Arabic.

The connection between the museums and the communities raises further questions. There are ethnic communities in Israel, mainly Jewish ones, which do not have museums. The most striking examples are Latin American Jewry and Russian Jewry and those from the Former Soviet Union. To them, one may add the communities of migrant workers in Israel, which currently numbers tens of thousands of residents and keeps on growing. The question posed is what does it mean that these communities are not represented in a museum framework? It may be that it is merely a question of time before such museums will be founded and that the delay has come about for technical reasons, such as problems of funding or simply no "fanatic devotee" has taken the issue in hand as yet. Yet, there is a possibility that the reason for the non-establishment of such museums is related to certain characteristics of the community or to the degree of its absorption or exclusion from Israeli society. Additionally, it may be that the role of the museum for these communities is played by another institution. Since this study only addressed existing museums, or those in the planning stages, such questions remain unanswered, but are deserving of discussion in future studies.

One last word remains about the ethnographic museum as an educational tool for the preservation of heritage in the future. While the older generation for each *edah* was included among the museum founders and the donors of objects, the main target audience has been the younger generation, unfamiliar with their parents' or grandparents' culture. A few museums were founded by people in the field of education, within schools or as part of another educational project. Examples are the Yemenite Jewish Heritage House in Rosh Haayin or the Museum for the Preservation of Bedouin Tradition in Segev Shalom. Other museums maintain contact with schools using other means. For example, in the Babylonian (Iraqi) Heritage Center there is an Education Department that actively deals with consolidating content suitable for children and markets the museum not only among families belonging to the community, but also to schools and youth movements. Operating in the Italian Jewish Museum is an educational unit that offers a variety of activity days for schools, including workshops for celebrating a bar mitzva in the style of Italian Jewry (Kessler, 2004, 52). The Circassian Museum in Rehaniya has an annual "Heritage Week" in conjunction with the local school (Hon, 30 January 2007). Thus, to a certain extent, the museums act as a substitute for the "elders of the community," as a social institution whose role is to maintain its heritage and bequeath it to future generations. The challenge of each ethnographic museum is to remain relevant for the coming generations even after the departure of the "fanatic devotee" who established it.

Bibliography

Abitbol, Michel. (1981). "Zionist Activity in North Africa until the End of World War II". In *North African Jews and Eretz Israel.* Edited by S. Bar-Asher and A. Maman. 119–29. Jerusalem: Beyahad.

Abu El-Haj, Nadia. (1988). "Translating Truths: Nationalism, the Practice of Archaeology, and the Remaking of Past and Present in Contemporary Jerusalem". *American Ethnologist* 25 (2): 166–88.

Administration of Society and Youth. (2008). "Examples of Achievements of the State" [in Hebrew]. Internet site of the Ministry of Education, http://noar. education.gov.il/main/upload/israel/tochnit5.doc.

Alexander, Edward Porter. (1979). *Museums in Motion: An Introduction to the History and Functions of Museums.* Nashville, Tenn.: Association for State and Local History.

Allen, Garth and Caroline Anson. (2005). *The Role of the Museum in Creating Multi-Cultural Identities: Lessons from Canada.* Lewiston, N.Y.: Edwin Mellen Press.

Ames, Michael M. (1992). *Cannibal Tours and Glass Boxes: The Anthropology of Museums.* Toronto: University of British Columbia Press.

Amitsur, Hagai. (2002). "General Survey" [in Hebrew]. In *Safed and Its Sites* (Ariel Nos. 157–158). Edited by Ely Schiller and Gavriel Barkay, 46–49. Jerusalem: Ariel.

Anderson, Benedict. (2006). *Imagined Communities.* 163–85. London and New York: Verso.

Anderson, Gail. (2004). "The Role of the Museum: The Challenge to Remain Relevant". In *Reinventing the Museum.* Edited by G. Anderson. 9–12. Walnut Creek, Calif.: AltaMira Press.

Ashkenazi, Eli. (2005, 3 Nov.) "Herzl and Hatikvah at the Thirtieth Anniversary of the Druze Zionist Movement" [in Hebrew]. *Haaretz.*

Atar, Ruth. (1991). "The Guidance at the 'Babylonian Jewry Museum'" [in Hebrew], *Nehardea* 9: 11–12.

Avishur, Yitzhak. (1989). "The Founding of the 'Babylonian Jewry Museum' and Illustration of Historical and Cultural Issues in It" [in Hebrew], *Nehardea* 7: 6–8.

Azaryahu, Maoz. (1995). *State Rites: The Celebration of Independence and Memorialization of the Fallen 1948–1956* [in Hebrew]. Beersheba: Ben-Gurion University.

Azoulay, Ariella. (1993). "Open Doors: Museums of History and the Israeli Public Space" [in Hebrew], *Theory and Criticism* 4: 81–82.

————. (1996). "Epilogue" [in Hebrew], *Studio*, 74: 1–2.

————. (1999). *Training for Art* [in Hebrew]. Tel Aviv: Hakibbutz Hameuhad.

Bachi, Gavriela. (1987). "Eretz Israel Museum" [in Hebrew]. In *Tel Aviv and Its Sites*. Edited by Gideon Biger and Ely Schiller. 177–84. Tel Aviv: Ariel.

Ballantyne, Roy and David Uzzell. (2011). "Looking Back and Looking Forward: The Rise of the Visitor-centered Museum", *Curator: The Museum Journal* 54 (1): 85–92.

Bar, Michael (1970). *Or Yehuda—Master Plan 1970–1972* (third booklet) [in Hebrew]. Tel Aviv, self-published.

Bar-Adon, D. K. (1941, 8 Sept.)"Palestine Folk Museum Reopened: New Quarters in Jerusalem Citadel". *Palestine Post.* 1.

Baram Ben-Yosef, Noam. (1997). *Draw Near, O Bride: Rituals for Betrothal and Marriage of the Jews of Afghanistan* [in Hebrew]. Jerusalem: Israel Museum.

Barkay, Gavriel. (1981a). "The Collections in the St. Etienne Monastery" [in Hebrew], *Kardom* 3 (16–17): 39–40.

————. (1981b). "The Russian-held Museum on the Mount of Olives" [in Hebrew], *Kardom* 3 (16–17): 41.

Bar-Levav, Avriel. (2002). "The Center for the Integration of the Heritage of Sephardic and Mizrahi Jews—From Idea to Institution: a Conversation with Nissim Yosha" [in Hebrew], *Pe'amim* 93: 157–71.

Bartal, Israel. (1976). "'Old Yishuv' and 'New Yishuv'—Image and Reality" [in Hebrew], *Cathedra* 2: 3–19.

"'Beit Hameiri'—The Museum and the Man" [in Hebrew]. (1987). *Moreshet Derekh* 19 (1987): 11.

Ben-Amos, Avner. (1995). "'Is Pluralism Impossible?' European and Oriental Jews in the History Curriculum in Israel" [in Hebrew]. In *Education toward the Twenty-first Century.* Edited by David Chen. 256–67. Tel Aviv: Ramot.

Ben-Amos, Avner and Ilana Bet-El. (1999). "Ceremonies, Education and History: Holocaust Memorial Day and Memorial Day for the Fallen in Israeli Schools" [in Hebrew]. In *Education and History: Cultural and Political Ties* Edited by Rivka Feldhay and Immanuel Etkes. 457–79. Jerusalem: Zalman Shazar Center.

Ben-Arieh, Yehoshua. (1977). *A City Reflected in Its Times: Jerusalem in the Nineteenth Century.* Part 1: The Old City [in Hebrew]. Jerusalem: Yad Ben-Zvi.

————. (1979). *A City Reflected in Its Times: Jerusalem in the Nineteenth Century.* Part 2: New Jerusalem: The Beginnings [in Hebrew]. Jerusalem: Yad Ben-Zvi.

———. (2000). "The Turkish Law on Archeological Excavations in Eretz Israel—1884" [in Hebrew]. In *Essays on Landscapes, Nature and Lore of Israel presented to Azaria Alon.* Edited by Gabriel Barkay and Ely Schiller,. 277–82. Jerusalem: Ariel.

———. (2001). "The Activity for the Preservation and Planning of Jerusalem at the Beginning of the British Mandate Period, 1917–1926" [in Hebrew]. In *A Land Reflected in Its Past, Studies in Historical Geography of Israel.* Edited by Ran Aaronsohn and Hagit Lavski. 447–554. Jerusalem: Magnes Press and Yad Ben-Zvi.

Ben-Porat, Mordechai. (1980). "The Way to Solve Israel's Social Problems" [in Hebrew], *Bamaaracha* 20 (239): 26.

———. (1993). "Babylonian Jewry Museum" [in Hebrew]. In *Jewish Ethnography in the Museum.* Edited by Avshalom Zemer. 33–35. Haifa: Association of Museums and ICOM Israel.

———. (1993). "The Babylonian Jewry Heritage Museum" [in Hebrew], *BaMuze'on* 6: 14–15.

———. (1996). *To Baghdad and Back* [in Hebrew]. Or Yehuda: Hed Arzi Publications.

Ben-Shalom, Shlomo, ed. (1975). *Words and Photos from the Association's Activity* [in Hebrew]. Netanya: Association for Fostering Society and Culture.

Ben-Yaakov, Avraham. (1980). *Babylonian Jews in Israel* [in Hebrew]. Jerusalem: Reuben Maas.

Benzur, Nina. (1985). "The Museum for Music and Ethnology" [in Hebrew]. In *Haifa and Its Sites.* Edited by Ely Schiller. 167–86. Jerusalem: Ariel.

Bialer, Yehuda Leib and Esther Fink. (1981). *A Mirror to Life in Jewish Art and Tradition* [in Hebrew]. Jerusalem: Hechal Shlomo.

Bier, Aharon. (1987). "Torah and Prayer Institutes between the Walls" [in Hebrew]. In *The Jewish Quarter in the Old City of Jerusalem.* Edited by Mordechai Naor. 127–48. Jerusalem: Company for the Renovation and Development of the Jewish Quarter in the Old City of Jerusalem.

Bliss, Frederick J. (1901). "Museum in Jerusalem", *PEFQS* 33: 209–10.

Brog, Mooly. (2003). "Victims and Victors: Holocaust and Military Commemoration in Israel", *Israel Studies* 8 (3): 65–99.

———. (2005). "Commemoration of the Holocaust in Cities and Settlements in Israel" [in Hebrew]. In *"Morning Will Rise Thanks to Their Blood": Memory and Commemoration in Israel* (Ariel 171–172). Edited by Ely Schiller and Gavriel Barkay. 175–80. Jerusalem: Ariel.

Cadaval, Olivia and Brian Finnegan. (2001). "'Our Voices in the Nation's Capital': Creating the Latino Community Heritage Center of Washington, D.C.", *Public Historian,* 23 (4): 73–90.

Cameron, Duncan. (1971). "The Museum, A Temple or the Forum", *Curator* 14 (1): 11–24.

Cannizzo, Jeanne. (1991). "Exhibiting Cultures: 'Into the Heart of Africa,'" *Visual Anthropology Review* 7 (1): 150–60.

Casey, Dawn. (2006). "Reflections of a National Museum Director". *In Memory, Monuments and Museums: The Past in the Present.* Edited by Marilyn Lake. 110–23. Carlton, Victoria: Melbourne University Publishing.

Chamberlain, Andrew. (1994). *Human Remains.* University of California Press.

Charmaz, Kathy. (2001). "Grounded Theory". In *Contemporary Field Research: Perspectives and Formulations.* Edited by Robert Emerson. 335–52. New York: Waveland.

Chetrit, Sami Shalom. (2004). *The Mizrahi Struggle in Israel: Between Oppression and Liberation, Identification and Alternative, 1948–2003* [in Hebrew]. Tel Aviv: Am Oved.

Cohen, Avraham Oded. (2002). "The Field of Heritage of Sephardic and Eastern Jewry—Interim Summary" [in Hebrew], *Pe'amim* 92: 5–8.

Cohen, Erik and Yosef Katan. (1966). *The Small Community in the Metropolitan Region* [in Hebrew]. Jerusalem: Hebrew University.

Cohen-Hattab, Kobi. (2006). *Tour the Land: Tourism in Palestine During the British Mandate Period 1917–1948* [in Hebrew]. Jerusalem: Yad Ben-Zvi.

Dahan-Kalev, Henriette. (2001). "Mizrahi Women: Identity and History" [in Hebrew]. In *Jewish Women in Pre-State Israel: Life History, Politics and Culture: A Gender Perspective,* edited by Margalit Shilo, Ruth Kark, and Galit Hasan-Rokem, 45–60. Jerusalem: Yad Ben-Zvi.

Dana, John Cotton. (1917). *The Gloom of the Museum.* Woodstock, Vt.: Elm Tree Press.

Darom, Naomi. "The Ability of Israel Museum's General Director" [in Hebrew], *The Marker Week,* 7 Aug. 2008.

[Davidovitch, David]. (1963). "Museum of Ethnography and Folklore" [in Hebrew], *Bulletin* (Eretz Israel Museum) 5: 17–19.

[———]. (1968). "Activity Report of Haaretz Museum" [in Hebrew], *Haaretz Museum Annual* 10: 57–63.

———, ed. (1971). *Memorial Exhibit: An-sky, Scholar of Jewish Folkore* [in Hebrew. Tel Aviv: Eretz Israel Museum.

———. (1976). "A Few Words on the Dedication of the Italian Synagogue Belonging to the Ethnography and Folklore Museum" [in Hebrew], *Yeda Am* 18 (43–44): 215–17.

Davis, Peter. (1999). *Ecomuseums: A Sense of Place.* London: Leicester University Press.

Davison, Graeme. (2006). "What Should a National Museum Do? Learning from the World". In *Memory, Monuments and Museums: The Past in the Present.* Edited by Marilyn Lake. 91–109. Carlton, Victoria: Melbourne University Publishing.

De Felice, Renzo. (1980). *Jews in an Arab Country: Libyan Jews between Colonialism, Arab Nationalism, and Zionism (1835–1970)* [in Hebrew]. Tel Aviv: Ma'ariv.

Department of Ethnography. (1971). *Beginnings and Hopes,* Jerusalem: Israel Museum.

Dicks, Bella. (2000). "Encoding and Decoding the People: Circuits of Communication at a Local Heritage Museum", *European Journal of Communication* 15 (1): 61–78.

Domínguez, Virginia R. (1989). *People as Subject, People as Object: Selfhood and Peoplehood in Contemporary Israel.* Madison, Wisc.: University of Wisconsin.

Dor-Shav, Ethan. (1998). "The Israel Museum and Loss of the Jewish Memory" [in Hebrew], *Tekhelet* 5: 103–13.

"The Dream and Its Realization: The Expansion Project of the Babylonian Jewry Center and Museum" [in Hebrew]. (1999). *Nehardea* 21: 27–32.

Doumani, Beshara B. (1992). "Rediscovering Ottoman Palestine: Writing Palestinians into History", *Journal of Palestine Studies* 21 (2): 5–28.

Duncan, Carol. (1994). "Art Museums and the Ritual of Citizenship". In *Interpreting Objects and Collections.* Edited by S. M. Pearce. 279–86. London and New York: Routledge.

Eisenstadt, Shmuel Noah. (2002). *Jewish Civilization* [in Hebrew]. Sdeh Boker: Ben-Gurion Heritage Center.

Editorial [in Hebrew]. (1993). *Ba-Muze'on* 6 : 1.

Education Committee of the International Committee for Museums. (1958). *Museums and Teachers* [in Hebrew]. Haifa: Museum of Ethnology and Folklore.

Eitan, H. Avi. (1988). "A Cornerstone for the Indian Jewry Heritage House in Haifa" [in Hebrew], *Ba-Ma'aracha* 329: 18.

El Khalidi, Leila. (1999). *The Art of Palestinian Embroidery.* London: Saqi Books.

Elgamil, Yosef. (1979). *History of Karaite Judaism* [in Hebrew]. Vol. 1. Ramleh: National Council of Karaite Jews in Israel, 1979.

Eliav, Mordechai. (1981). "The Jewish Yishuv in Jerusalem toward the End of the Ottoman Period (1815–1914)". In *Jerusalem in the Modern Period* [in Hebrew]. Edited by Eli Shaltiel. 133–35. Jerusalem: Yad Ben Zvi.

Ettinger, Yair. (2006, 21 Apr.). "The Mimouna in an Identity Crisis: No Longer a Symbol of the Folk", *Haaretz.*

Exhibition of Palestine crafts and industries held in the Citadel [catalogue]. (1922). Jerusalem.

"'The Farhud'—Part of the Holocaust" [in Hebrew]. (2005). *Nehardea* 15 : 5.

Fenichel, Deborah. (2005). "Exhibiting Ourselves as Others: Jewish Museums in Israel". Ph.D. diss. Indiana University.

Finn, Elizabeth Anne. (1892). "Notes and News", *Palestine Exploration Fund Quarterly Statement* 24: 266.

Finn, J. (1980). *Stirring Times: Or Records from Jerusalem Consular Chronicles of 1853 to 1856* [in Hebrew]. Vol. 2. Jerusalem: Yad Ben-Zvi.

Fishof, Iris. (1982). "The Nahon Italian Jewish Museum" [in Hebrew]. In *Jerusalem and Its Sites* (Hoveret Kardom 21–23). Edited by Ely Schiller. 141–43. Jerusalem: Ariel.

Foucault, Michel. (1986). "Of Other Spaces", *Diacritics* 16 (1): 22–27.

Frost, Yossi. (1993). "Community Museums in Israel and the Link to the Communities in the Dispersal" [in Hebrew], *BaMuzeʾon* 6: 2.

Fuller, Nancy J. (1992). "The Museum as a Vehicle for Community Empowerment: The Ak-Chin Indian Community Ecomuseum Project". In *Museums and Communities*. Edited by Ivan Karp, Christine Mullen Kreamer, and Steven Levine. 327–65. Washington, D.C.: Smithsonian Institution Press.

Gaither, Edmund Barry. (1992). "'Hey! That's Mine': Thoughts on Pluralism and American Museums". In *Museums and Communities*. Edited by Ivan Karp, Christine Mullen Kreamer, and Steven Levine. Washington, D.C.: Smithsonian Institution Press.

Gavish, Galya. (1994). "The Museum in an Ancient Structure" [in Hebrew], *Ba-Muzeʾon* 9: 8–9.

Gian, Baruch. (2000). "Alhambra in Jerusalem" [in Hebrew], *Eretz ve-Teva* 69: 22. 16–22.

Gillerman, Dana. (2006, 4 Sept.). "Some People Claim We Stole Their Heritage" [in Hebrew], *Haaretz*, 4 Sep 2006.

"The 'Ginza' Circle and Its Activities" [in Hebrew]. (1961). *Bulletin* (Eretz Israel Museum) 3: 18–19.

"Ginza—Museum for Jewish Folk Art" [in Hebrew]. (1962). *Bulletin* (Eretz Israel Museum) 4: 17.

Glaser, Barney G. and Anselm I. Strauss. (1967). *The Discovery of Grounded Theory: Strategies for Qualitative Research.* Chicago: Aldine.

Glock, Albert. (1994). "Archaeology as Cultural Survival: The Future of the Palestinian Past", *Journal of Palestinian Studies* 23 (3): 70–84.

Goldmann, Nahum. (1972). *Memoirs* [in Hebrew]. Jerusalem: Weidenfeld & Nicolson.

———. (1996). "Bridge between Israel and the Diaspora" [in Hebrew]. In *Beit Hatfutsot.* Edited by Idit Zartal. Tel Aviv: Beit Hatfutsot.

Goldstein, Kaylin. (2003). "On Display: The Politics of Museums in Israeli Society". Ph.D. diss. University of Chicago.

———. (2005). "Secular Sublime: Edward Said at the Israel Museum", *Public Culture* 17 (1): 27–53.

Gonen, Rivka, ed. (1994). *Back to the Shtetl* [in Hebrew]. Jerusalem: Israel Museum.

Goren, Haim, ed. (1999). *"Go View the Land": German Study of Palestine in the Nineteenth Century* [in Hebrew]. Jerusalem: Yad Izhak Ben-Zvi.

Gwyneira, Isaac. "Mediating Knowledges: Zuni Negotiations for a Culturally Relevant Museum", *Museum Anthropology* 28 (1): 3.

Hacohen, Devora. (1994). *Immigrants in Turmoil: Mass Immigration and Its Absorption in Israel 1948–1953* [in Hebrew]. Jerusalem: Yad Ben-Zvi.

Hacohen, Moshe. (1989). "A Center for the Heritage of North African Jewry Will Be Created in the Center of Jerusalem" [In Hebrew]. *Ba-Ma'aracha* 339–341: 26.

Hakiwai, Arapata T. (2005). "The Search for Legitimacy: Museums in Aotearoa, New Zealand—a Maori Viewpoint". In *Heritage, Museums and Galleries: An Introductory Reader.* Edited by G. Corsane. 154–62. London and New York: Routledge.

Hamdan, Taha. (2001). "The History and Role of Museum in Palestine", *ICOM Study Series* 9: 25–27.

Hammer, Juliane. (2005). *Palestinians Born in Exile: Diaspora and the Search for a Homeland.* Austin: University of Texas Press.

Hasan-Rokem, Galit. (1977). "On the Study of Folk Culture" [in Hebrew], *Theory and Criticism* 10: 5–13.

Hazan, Uziel. (2001). *The Mahane Israel Neighborhood: The First Neighborhood Outside the Walls of Jerusalem That Was Founded at the Initiative of Individuals* [in Hebrew]. Jerusalem: World Center for North African Jewish Heritage.

Heritage Center for Druze in Israel Law, 5767–2007 [in Hebrew].

Herreman, Yani. (2006). "The Role of Museums Today: Tourism and Cultural Heritage". In *Art and Cultural Heritage: Law, Policy and Practice*. Edited by Barbara T. Hoffman. 419–26. Cambridge: Cambridge University Press.

Hooper-Greenhill, Eilean. (1994). *Museums and Their Visitors*. London and New York: Routledge.

Horowitz, Tamar. [1991]. "Awareness without Legitimacy: Responses of the Israeli Education System to Intercultural Differences" [in Hebrew], *Iyunim beHinukh* 55: 13–14.

Howard, Peter. (2002). "The Eco-museum: Innovation That Risks the Future", *International Journal of Heritage Studies* 8 (1): 63–72.

Hoyt, Marilyn C. (1996). "Community-Based Museums: Past, Present, and Future", *Curator* 39 (2): 90–93.

Hysler-Rubin, Noah. (2005). "Planning the Artistic City: Charles Robert Ashbee in Jerusalem 1918–1922" [in Hebrew], *Cathedra* 117 (2005): 81–102.

ICOM Statutes, Article 3, Paragraph 1 http://icom.museum/statutes.html

Inbar, Yehudit and Ely Schiller, eds. (1995). *Museums in Israel: New Updated and Expanded Edition* [in Hebrew]. Jerusalem: Ariel.

"Initial Steps Have Been Taken to Recruit Support for the Founding of a Museum of Samaritan Heritage in Holon" [in Hebrew]. (1990). *A. B. Hadashot* 513:4.

"In Kiryat Luza Arrangements Are Beginning to Be Made toward Establishing the First Samaritan Museum" [in Hebrew]. (1993). *A.B. Hadashot* 588–589: 5.

Itzkowitz, Natalya Berger. (2006). "Between Past and Present: The Jewish Museum as a Mirror for Processes of the Consolidation of Jewish Identity in Modern Times" [in Hebrew]. Ph.D. diss. Hebrew University of Jerusalem.

Izraeli, Dafna. (1993). "They have eyes and see not: Gender politics in the diaspora museum", *Psychology of Women Quarterly* 17: 515–23.

Jablonka, Hanna. (2008). *Far From the Track: The Mizrahim and the Holocaust*. Tel Aviv: Yediot Ahronot and Ben-Gurion University of the Negev.

Joint Committee of the Aliyah, Absorption, and Diaspora Affairs Committee and the Knesset Financial Committee on the topic of proposing a bill for the study of the heritage of Ethiopian Jewry 5759-1999. Protocol of meeting no. 1 [in Hebrew]. (2001, 6 Mar.).

Jones, D. Gareth and Robyn J. Harris. (1998). "CA Forum on Anthropology in Public: Archeological Human Remains: Scientific, Cultural, and Ethical Considerations", *Current Anthropology* 39 (2): 253–64.

Juhasz, Esther. (1989). *The Jews of Spain in the Ottoman Empire: Aspects of Material Culture* [in Hebrew]. Jerusalem: Israel Museum.

Kamal, Zahira. (1998). "The Development of the Palestinian Women's Movement". In *Palestinian Women of Gaza and the West Bank.* Edited by Suha Sabbagh, 78–88. Bloomington, Ind.: Indiana University Press.

Kark, Ruth. (1984). "The Moghrabim—The First Jerusalemites in the Building of a Neighborhood Outside the Wall" [in Hebrew], *Pe'amim* 21: 20–30.

———. (1991a). "A Pioneering Neighborhood of Members of the Moghrabi Community in New Jerusalem: 'Mahane Israel' and Rabbi Tzuf Devash" [in Hebrew]. In *Pioneers with Weeping: Selected Issues about North African Jewry.* Edited by Shimon Shitrit. 66–83. Tel Aviv: Am Oved.

———. (1991b). "On Birds and Object from the Holy Land to America: Collections of the Consul Sela Merril and His Contemporaries" [in Hebrew]. In *Essays on Landscapes, Nature and Lore of Israel presented to Azaria Alon.* Edited by Gavriel Barkay and Ely Schiller. 243–49. Jerusalem: Am Oved.

——— and Noam Perry (2008). "Museums and Multiculturalism in Israel" [in Hebrew], *Ofakim ba-Geografiya* 70: 105–161.

Karp, Ivan. (1992). "Introduction: Museum and Communities: The Politics of Public Culture". In *Museum and Communities.* Edited by Ivan Karp, Christine Mullen Kreamer, and Steven D. Lavine. Washington: Smithsonian Institution Press.

Katriel, Tamar. (1992). "The Past as a Distant Country—Historical Museums versus Ethnographic Museums" [in Hebrew]. In *Jewish Ethnography in the Museum* [in Hebrew]. Tel Aviv: Israeli chapter of ICOM.

———. (1997). "To Tell about the Land of Israel: Ethnography of the Museum for the History of Settlement" [in Hebrew], *Devarim Ahadim* 2: 56–78.

Katz, Karl. (1968). "Background to a Museum". In *From the Beginning: Archaeology and Art in the Israel Museum,* Jerusalem. Edited by Karl Katz, Penuel P. Kahane, and Magen Broshi. 11–31. New York: William Morrow and Company.

———. (1968). "World Art in Jerusalem". In *From the Beginning: Archaeology and Art in the Israel Museum,* Jerusalem. Edited by Karl Katz, Penuel P. Kahane, and Magen Broshi, 216–73. New York: William Morrow and Company.

Kawar, Amal. (1996). *Daughters of Palestine: Leading Women of the Palestinian National Movement.* Albany: State University of New York.

Kawar, Widad Kamel, and Tania Nasir. (1980). "The Traditional Palestinian Costume", *Journal of Palestine Studies* 10 (1): 118–29.

Kelly, Lynda, Allison Bartlett, and Phil Gordon. (2002). *Indigenous Youth and Museums*. Sydney: Australian Museum.

Kessler, Nava. (2004). "Museum of Italian Jewry" [in Hebrew], *Etrog* 22 (2004): 52–53.

Kletter, Raz. (2006). *Just Past. The Making of Israeli Archaeology*. London: Equinox.

Klorman, Bat-Zion Eraqi. (2006). "Yemeni Jewish Historiography and the Formation of National Identity" [in Hebrew]. In *To Invent a Nation* [in Hebrew]. 299–330. Raanana: Open University.

Knesset Absorption and Diaspora Affairs Committee, Protocol of meeting no. 113 [in Hebrew]. (2000, 27 Nov.).

Knesset Committee for Immigration, Absorption and Diaspora Affairs. Protocol of meeting no. 216. (2008, 7 July).

Knesset Economics Committee. Protocol of meeting no. 446 [in Hebrew]. (2005, 19 July).

Knesset Economics Committee. Protocol of meeting no. 536 [in Hebrew]. (2005, 28 Nov.).

Knesset Education and Culture Committee. Protocol of meeting 242 [in Hebrew]. (2001, 20 Feb.).

Knesset Education and Culture Committee. Protocol of meeting no. 239 [in Hebrew]. (2001, 11 June).

Knesset Education, Culture, and Sport Committee. Protocol of meeting no. 128 [in Hebrew]. (2007, 29 Kark, Ruth and Noam Perry (2008). "Museums and Multiculturalism in Israel" [in Hebrew], *Ofakim ba-Geografiya* 70: 105–161.

Kol-Inbar, Yehudit. (1992). "History of the Museums in Eretz Israel until the establishment of the State [of Israel] as an expression of the Zionist Vision" [in Hebrew]. Master's Thesis, Hebrew University of Jerusalem.

Kollek, Teddy, et al. (1990). "Museums and the National Spirit" (a symposium held at the Israel Museum on its twenty-fifth anniversary…) [in Hebrew], Studio 15: 41–49.

Lahav, Pnina. (2006). "A Chandelier for Woman: A Tale about the Diaspora Museum and Maurycy Gottlieb's Day of Atonement—Jews Praying on Yom Kippur", *Israel Studies* 11 (1): 108–42.

Lancet, Aviva, ed. (1958). *Folkore of Minorities in Israel Exhibit* [in Hebrew]. Acre: Interior Ministry and Acre Municipal Museum.

Levi, Itamar. (1996). "The Story of the Israel Museum" [in Hebrew]. *Studio* 72: 4–5.

Levi-Barzilai, Vered. (2004, 9 July). "By the way, Mendel opened a museum" [in Hebrew], *Haaretz Supplement.*

Liebman, Yeshayahu. (1981). "The Holocaust Myth in Israeli Society" [in Hebrew], *Tefutsot Israel* 19 (5–6): 101–14.

Lifschitz, Alona and Ely Schiller. (1995). "General Survey" [in Hebrew]. In *Museums in Israel: New Updated and Expanded Edition,* 269–72. Jerusalem: Ariel.

Low, Theodore. (2004). "What Is a Museum?", reprinted in *Reinventing the Museum: Historical and Contemporary Perspectives on the Paradigm Shift.* Edited by Gail Anderson. 30–43. Walnut Creek, Calif.: AltaMira Press.

Lukin, Binyamin. (1994). "From Folkness to a People—An-sky's Way in Jewish Ethnography" [in Hebrew]. In *Back to the Shtetl.* Edited by Rivka Gonen. 27–40. Jerusalem: Israel Museum.

Luncz, Avraham Moshe. (5661 [1901]). "The General Beit Atikot in Jerusalem" [in Hebrew], *Jerusalem Almanac.* Year 7: 171–72.

Luxembourg, Daniella, ed. (1981). *The Old Yishuv Court.* Jerusalem: Old Yishuv Court Museum.

———. (1981). "Introduction" [in Hebrew]. In *The Old Yishuv Court.* Edited by Daniella Luxembourg. Jerusalem: Old Yishuv Court Museum.

Makuvaza, Simon. (2002). "Towards a new type of 'ethnographic' museum in Africa", paper presented at the annual conference of the International Committee for Museums of Ethnography (ICME), Zambia.

Martyrs' and Heroes Remembrance (*Yad Vashem*) Law 5713–1953 [in Hebrew].

Medad, H. (1988). "Babylonian Jewry Pays Tribute to the Past: the Museum of Babylonian Jewry Has Been Founded in Or Yehuda" [in Hebrew], *Bama'aracha: Journal of the Sephardic and Oriental Jewish Communities* 330 (1): 14.

Meir-Glitzenstein, Esther. (2000). "Iraqi Immigrants and the Israeli Establishment in the Early 1950s" [in Hebrew]. In *The Zionist Era.* Jerusalem: Zalman Shazar Center.

———. (2004). "Zionist Identity and Jewish-Arab Identity in the Collective Memory of Iraqi Immigrants in Israel" [in Hebrew], *Alpayim* 27: 173–202.

Merriman, Nick and Nima Poovaya-Smith. (1996). "Making Culturally Diverse Histories". In *Making Histories in Museums.* Edited by G. Kavanagh. 176–87. London and New York: Leicester University Press.

Mikdash-Shamailov, Liya, ed. (2001). *Mountain Jews: Customs and Daily Life in the Caucasus* [in Hebrew]. Jerusalem: Israel Museum.

Ministry of Justice, Museums Law, 5743-1983 [in Hebrew].

Mizrahi, Avshalom, ed. (1997). *An Association and Its Mission* [in Hebrew]. Netanya: Association for Fostering Society and Culture.

———, ed. (2001). *Edot—Edot le-Yisra'el: Diaspora, Aliyot, Absorption, and Merging* [in Hebrew]. Netanya: Association for Fostering Society and Culture, Documentation and Research.

———. (2000). *On an Unpaved Road: A Life's Path and a Life's Work* [in Hebrew]. Netanya: Association for Fostering society and Culture, Documentation and Research.

Mor, Yehudit. (2003). "The Bet Hameiri Museum" [in Hebrew]. In *Safed and Its Sites* (Ariel Nos. 157–158) [in Hebrew]. Edited by Ely Schiller and Gavriel Barkay. 195–98. Jerusalem: Ariel.

Mouchon, Levana. (2007). "A Museum for Jewish Heritage in Israel" [in Hebrew], *Etrog: Journal for Education, Judaism and Society* 34: 40–45.

Muchawsky-Schnapper, Esther, ed. (1991). *The Jews of Alsace: Village, Tradition, Emancipation* [in Hebrew]. Jerusalem: Israel Museum.

———, ed. (2000). *The Jews of Yemen: Two Thousand Years of Jewish Culture* [in Hebrew]. Jerusalem: Israel Museum.

(Muller-Lancet, Aviva, ed.). 1968. *Bukhara.* Israel Museum, Jerusalem.

———. (1974). "Exhibition and Ethnic Image", paper presented at the annual conference of the International Committee for Museums of Ethnography (ICME), Denmark.

———, ed. (1973). *Jewish Life in Morocco* [in Hebrew]. Jerusalem: Israel Museum.

———. (1978). "Toward the Kurdistan Exhibit" [in Hebrew], *Hithadshut* 3: 175–77.

———. (1993). "Idéal ethnologique et réalité muséographique en Israël". In Ferreurs contemporaine: *Textes d'anthropologie urbaine offerts a Jacques Gutwirth.* Edited by Colette Péttonet et Yves Delaporte. 287–302. Paris: L'Harmattan.

Murphy, Bernice L. (2004). "The Definition of the Museum: From Specialist Reference to Social Recognition and Service", *ICOM News* 2 (2004): 3.

Murray, David. (1904). Museums, *Their History and Their Use: With a Bibliography and List of Museums in the United Kingdom.* Glasgow: J. MacLehose and Sons.

"A Museum for Ethiopian Jewish Heritage Will Be Built in Rehovot" [in Hebrew]. (2002, 9 July). *Hatzofeh.*

Nahon, Shlomo Umberto. (1970). *Torah Arks and Ritual Objects from Italy in Israel* [in Hebrew]. Tel Aviv: Dvir.

Nassar, Issam. (2006). "Thoughts on Writing the History of Palestinian Identity" [in Hebrew]. In *Inventing a Nation.* Edited by Yossi Dahan and Henry Wasserman. 142–56. Ra'anana: Open University.

Naveh, Eyal and Esther Yogev. (2002). *Histories—Towards a Dialogue with the Israeli Past* [in Hebrew]. 28–46. Tel Aviv: Babel.

Navon, Avi. (1988). "The Center Named for Joe Alon" [in Hebrew]. In *Guide to Kibbutz Museums.* Edited by Eli Schiller. 105–8. Jerusalem: Ariel.

Nevo, Ra'aya. (1981). "Here History Is Presented like a Novel, Not like a Textbook" [in Hebrew], *Otot* 34: 23.

Noble, Joseph Veach. (1970). "Museum Manifesto", *Museum News* (April): 27–32.

Noriega, Chon A. (1999). "On Museum Row: Aesthetics and the Politics of Exhibition (museum vs. the state since the 1980s)", *Daedalus* 128 (3): 57–82.

Noy, Dov. (2002). *The Iriquois: Guide to an Exhibition of an Indian Tribe in the United States* [in Hebrew]. Jerusalem: Ariel.

———. (1977–78). "The Haifa Archive for the Folktale in Israel" [in Hebrew]. *Karmelit* 21–22: 259–62.

"Opening for the General Public" [in Hebrew]. (2005). *Arkadaş —The Turkish Community in Israel Association* 6: 10.

Orman, Dan. (1983). "History of Akko in the Ottoman Period", *Kardom* (Acre and Its Sites) 24–25: 40–58.

Oved, Moshe. (1981). *The Story of an Ethnic Group: Yemenite Jewry* [in Hebrew]. Jerusalem: Ministry of Education and Culture—The Center for the Integration of the Heritage of Mizrahi Jewry.

Oz, Amos. (1979). *Under This Blazing Light: Articles and Essays* [in Hebrew]. Tel Aviv: Hakibbutz Haartzi.

Pachter, Marc. "Why Museums Matter". In *Museums in the Digital Age.* Edited by Ross Parry. 332–35. London and New York: Routledge.

Perin, Constance. (1992). "The Communicative Circle: Museums as Communities". In *Museums and Communities.* Edited by Ivan Karp, Christine Mullen Kreamer, and Steven D. Lavine. 182–220. Washington, D.C.: Smithsonian Institution Press.

Perry, Noam. (2007). "The First Museums in Jerusalem: Their Beginning and Their End" [in Hebrew], final paper for the course "Research Camp", Hebrew University of Jerusalem.

Porat, Dina. (2000). *Beyond the Material—The Biography of Abba Kovner* [in Hebrew]. Tel Aviv: Am Oved.

Porat, Yehuda. (2006). "The Role of Ethnic Museums in Multicultural Israeli Society: The Museum for the Commemoration of Hungarian Speaking Jewry" [in Hebrew], final paper for the course Local Museology and Methodology for Archival Research, Hebrew University of Jerusalem.

Poulot, Dominque. (1994). "Identity as Self-Discovery: The Ecomusuem in France". In *Museum Culture: Histories, Discourses, Spectacles.* Edited by Daniel J. Sherman and Irit Rogoff. 66–84. Minneapolis: University of Minnesota Press.

Rabinowitz, Ronit. (1989). "The Family Section" [in Hebrew], *BaMuze'on* 2: 8–12.

Rahmani, Levi Yizhaq. 1976. *The Museums of Israel.* New York: Rizzoli.

Ram, Uri. (2006). *Time of the "Post": Nationalism and the Politics of Knowledge in Israel* [in Hebrew]. Tel Aviv: Riesling, 2006.

Rapp, David. (2005, 15 Apr.). "Excuse me, where's the museum here?" [in Hebrew]. *Haaretz Weekly Supplement.* 58–63.

Rappaport, Meron. (2008, 11 Apr.). "Excavations War" [in Hebrew], *Weekly Haaretz.*

Raz-Krakotzkin, Amnon. (1993). "Exile within Sovereignty: On Criticism of 'Negating the Diaspora' in Israeli Culture (Part One)" [in Hebrew], *Theory and Criticism,* 3: 23–55.

———. (1994) "Exile within Sovereignty: On Criticism of 'Negating the Diaspora' in Israeli Culture (Part Two)" [in Hebrew], *Theory and Criticism,* 5: 113–32.

"Review of the Museum's Activities in 1976–1983" [in Hebrew]. (1983/4). *Israel— Am va-Aretz* A, 19: 265–82.

Rios-Bustamente, Antonio and Christine Marin, eds. (1998). *Latinos in Museums: A Heritage Reclaimed.* Malabar, Fla.: Krieger Publishing Company,

Romano, Giorgio. (1978). "Shlomo Umberto Nahon" [in Hebrew]. *Sefer Zikkaron li-Shlomo Umberto Nahon: A collection of articles on the history of Italian Jewry.* Edited by Robert Bonfil et al. 13–34. Jerusalem: Sally Mayer Foundation.

Rousso, Liat. (2004). "Background Document: Museum Budget" [Hebrew]. Internet site of the Knesset Research and Information Center. http://www.knesset.gov.il/MMM/data/docs/m0122.doc.

Rozovsky, Nitza and Joy Ungerleider-Mayerson. (1989). *The Museums of Israel.* New York: Abrams Publishers.

Rubinstein-Cohen, Claire. (2005). *Painters of Tunisia: Impressions and Colors.* Jerusalem: Worldwide North Africa Jewish Heritage Center.

Rudin, Nina. (1995). "Museums in Split Societies (News from the Museum)" [in Hebrew], *Ba-Muze'on* 11: 26–27.

———. (1998). "The Settlement Museums of Israel and Their Commitment to Zionist Messages". M.A. Thesis, University of Leicester.

Ruffins, Faith D. (1992). "Mythos, Memory and History: African American Preservation Efforts, 1820–1990". In *Museums and Communities.* Edited by Ivan Karp, Christine Mullen Kreamer, and Steven D. Lavine. 555–70. Washington, D.C.: Smithsonian Institution Press.

Sa'di, Ahmad H. (2002). "Catastrophe, Memory and Identity: Al-Nakba as a Component of Palestinian Identity", *Israel Studies* 7 (2): 175–98.

Salameh, Khader. (2001). *The Qur'an Manuscripts in the Al-Haram Al-Sharif Islamic Museum Jerusalem.* Paris: Garnet & Ithaca Press.

Sanbato, Ayna'o P. (2006, 10 Mar.) "Operation Moses" [in Hebrew], *Haaretz Weekly Supplement.*

Saraf, Michal. (1979). "Tunisian Emigrés Are Setting Out to Reveal the Roots of Their Culture and Heritage" [in Hebrew]. *Ba-Ma'aracha* 226: 17.

———. (1989). "Habermann Institute for Literary Research" [in Hebrew]. *Apiryon* 13: 37–40.

Schiller, Ely. (1980). "The Bethlehem Museum" [in Hebrew]. In *Bethlehem and the Church of the Nativity.* Edited by Ely Schiller. Jerusalem: Ariel.

———. (1981). "The Armenian Museum" [in Hebrew], *Kardom* 3 (nos. 16–17): 24–26.

———. (1990). "About Forty New Museums Will Be Established in Israel in the Coming Years (a collection of items)" [in Hebrew]. In *Jerusalem and Eretz Israel* Edited by Ely Schiller and Gideon Biger. 246. Jerusalem: Ariel.

Schwartz-Be'eri, Ora, ed. (1982). *Jews of Kurdistan: Way of Life, Tradition, and Art.* Jerusalem: Israel Museum.

Sciolino, Elaine. (2007, 26 Oct.). "French Debate: Is Maori Head Body Part or Art?", *New York Times—Europe.*

Shaham, Pnina. (2005). "Important to Know: About the Guidance Activity" [in Hebrew], *Nehardea* 27: 47.

Shahar, Eitan and Leah Cacen. (2008). "Adjustment of Cochin Immigrants Who Settled in Moshav Nevatim in the Negev" [in Hebrew]. In *Beersheba: A Metropolis in Formation.* Edited by Yehuda Gradus and Esther Meir-Glitzenstein. 125–43. Beersheba: Ben-Gurion University.

Shai, Oded. (2006). "Beginnings of Museums and Collections in Eretz Israel at the End of the Ottoman Period (1848–1917)" [in Hebrew]. Ph.D. diss., Bar-Ilan University.

Shalev-Khalifa, Nurit. (2006). *Hidden Treasures of Israel* [in Hebrew]. Tel Aviv: Mapa.

Shapira, Anita. (1997). "*Ben-Gurion* and the *Bible*: The Forging of an Historical Narrative?" [in Hebrew], Alpayim 14: 207–31.

Sharoni, Idit. (1990). "An Exhibition of Hanukkah Menorahs from Babylonia" [in Hebrew], *Nehardea* 8: 31–32.

———. (1991). "The Collections of Objects in the 'Center'" [in Hebrew]. *Nehardea* 9: 13.

Shelton, Anthony Alan. (2006). "Museums and Anthropologies: Practices and Narratives". In *A Companion to Museum Studies*. Edited by Sharon MacDonald. Malden, Mass. and Oxford, UK: Blackwell.

Shenhav-Keller, Shelly. (2005). "'All This Lie, It's All True'—Objects, Displays, and Past in Bet Hatfutsot" [in Hebrew], *Motar* 13: 13–22.

Shibli, Diyab. (1992). *Galilee Bedouins* [in Hebrew]. Tel Aviv: Integrated Pedagogical Center.

Shiloni, Israel. (1998). *Possible and Impossible: Memoirs* [in Hebrew]. Tefen: Open Museum, Industrial Garden.

Shimshoni, Daniel. (2002). *Rosh Ha'ayin: From an Immigrant Camp to a Thriving City* [in Hebrew]. Jerusalem: Magnes Press.

Simpson, Moira G. (2001). *Making Representations: Museums in the Post-Colonial Era* (rev. ed.). London and New York: Routledge.

Shohat, Ella, ed. (2001). "Split Identity: Thoughts of an Arab-Jewish Woman". In *Tabu Memories: Toward Multicultural Thought* [in Hebrew]. Edited by E. Shohat. 242–51. Tel Aviv: Bimat Kedem le-Sifrut.

Skramstad, Harold. (1999). "An Agenda for American Museums in the Twenty-First Century", *Daedalus*, 128 (3): 109–28.

Slapak, Orpa, ed. (1995). *Jews of India: Bene Israel–Cochin–Baghdadi* [in Hebrew]. Jerusalem: Israel Museum.

Sowayan, Saad A. (1993). "Forward", *Asian Folklore Studies* 52: 1–3.

Stark, Chareen. (2008). "The Legacy of Hind al-Husseini", *Washington Report on Middle East Affairs*, 27 (4): 19–20.

Stern, Ephraim and Hanan Eshel, eds. (2002). *Sefer ha-Shomronim*. Jerusalem: Yad Ben-Zvi.

Stern, Yoav. (2008, 3 Feb.). "If There's Already a Sign in the Park—the Destroyed Palestinian Village Will Also Be Mentioned" [in Hebrew]. *Haaretz*.

Suarez, Freya et al., eds. [1960]. *Libyan Jewry* [in Hebrew]. Tel Aviv: Committee of Libyan Communities in Israel.

Sussman, Ayala, and Ronny Reich. (1987). "The History of the Rockefeller Museum" [in Hebrew]. In *Zev Vilnay's Jubilee* Volume II, edited by Ely Schiller, 83–92. Jerusalem, Ariel.

Tal, Miriam. (1966). "Is the Israel Museum a National Museum?" [in Hebrew]. *Haumah* 4 (16): 564–61.

Tamir, Tali. (1990). "The Israel Museum: From Dream to Fulfillment", *Israel Museum Journal*, 9: 7–16.

Toledano, Joe (exhibit curator). (2005). *Figures in the History of Moroccan Jewry from Their Earliest Settlement Through Today* [in Hebrew]. Jerusalem: Worldwide North Africa Jewish Heritage Center.

Turel, Sarah. (2013). *Ethiopia: Journey to Wonderland* [in Hebrew]. Tel Aviv: Eretz Israel Museum.

Tzaferis, Vasilis. (1985). *Museum of the Greek Orthodox Patriarchate of Jerusalem* [in Hebrew], Jerusalem: self-published.

Tzuriel, Shaked. (1960). "Libyan Immigrants in Settlement" [in Hebrew]. In *Libyan Jewry.* Edited by F. Suarez et al. 325–42. Tel Aviv: Committee of Libyan Communities in Israel.

UNESCO. 1998. *Statistical Yearbook.* Paris.

Van Gulik, Willem. (1989). "Von Siebold and His Japanese Collection in Leiden". In *Leiden Oriental Connections 1850–1940.* Edited by W. Otterspeer. 378–91. Leiden and New York: E. J. Brill.

Veil, Stephen E. (2004). "Rethinking the Museum: An Emerging New Paradigm", reprinted in *Reinventing the Museum.* Edited by Gail Anderson. 74–79. Walnut Creek, Calif.: AltaMira Press.

Vilnay, Zev. (1970). *Jerusalem Capital of Israel: The Old City* [in Hebrew]. Vol. 1. Jerusalem: Achiever.

———. (1974). *Jerusalem Capital of Israel: The New City* [in Hebrew]. Vol. 3. Jerusalem: Achiever.

Walerstein, Marcia Shoshana. 1987. "Public Rituals among the Jews from Cochin, India in Israel: Expressions of Ethnic Identity". Ph. diss., University of California, Los Angeles.

Walsh, Kevin. (1992). *The Representation of the Past: Museums and Heritage in the Post-Modern World.* London: Routledge.

Weil, Stephen. (1999). "From Being about Something to Being for Somebody: The Ongoing Transformation of the American Museum", *Daedalus,* 128 (3): 229–58.

Weinberg, Jesaya. (1989). "A Different Kind of Museum" [in Hebrew], *Ba-Muze'on* 2: 7–8.

Weingarten, Rivka. (1981). "The 'Or ha-Hayyim' Court" [in Hebrew]. In *The Old Yishuv Court.* Edited by Daniella Luxembourg. n.p., Jerusalem: Old Yishuv Court Museum.

Weingarten, Rivka. (1987). "And These Are the Roots ..." [in Hebrew]. In *In the Service of Jerusalem: The History of the Pach Rosenthal Family 1839–1926.* By Arie Morganstern. 8–11. Jerusalem: self-published.

Weyl, Martin. (1996). "The Story of the Israel Museum" [in Hebrew], *Studio* 73: 4.

Wigoder, Geoffrey, ed. (n.d.). *Beit Hatfutsot—The Early Years* [in Hebrew]. n.p.

Yahel, H. Perry, N., and Kark, R., Keynote Paper: "Multiculturalism and Ethnographic Museums in Israel: The Case of a Regional Bedouin Museum", ICME (ICOM) conference on "Museums and Cultural Landscapes. Curating and Engaging: Peoples, Places and Entanglements in an Age of Migrations", Milan, Italy, July 2016.

Yair, Orna. (2004). "Types of Museums in Israel" [in Hebrew]. Ph.D. diss., Hebrew University of Jerusalem.

Yardai, Efrat. (2013, 20 Mar.) "To Uncover the Truth about Ethiopian Jewry" [in Hebrew]. *Haaretz.*

Yehuda, Zvi. (1990). "The Opening of the 'Sport Wing' in Jewish Schools in Iraq" [in Hebrew], *Nehardea* 8: 30–31.

———. (1991). "The Research Infrastructure of the 'Center'" [in Hebrew], *Nehardea* 9: 16–17.

———. (1992). "The Stores of the Silversmith in 'The Lane'–Design and Research" [in Hebrew]. *Nehardea* 10: 9–10.

———. (2002). "Changes among Baghdad Jewry in the Twelfth to Eighteenth Centuries" [in Hebrew]. In *Studies in the History and Culture of the Jews in Babylonia.* Edited by Yitzhak Avishur and Zvi Yehuda. 9–29. Or Yehuda: Babylonian Jewry Heritage Center.

Yonah, Yossi. (2005). *In Virtue of Difference: The Multicultural Project in Israel* [in Hebrew]. Jerusalem: Hakibbutz Hameuchad.

Zameret, Zvi. (1997). *Across a Narrow Bridge: Shaping the Education System during the Great Aliya* [in Hebrew]. Sdeh Boker: Ben-Gurion Research Center.

Zandberg, Esther. (2008, 24 July). "It's Your Problem" [in Hebrew], *Haaretz—Gallery.*

———. (2007, 25 June). "New Order in the Museum" [in Hebrew], *Haaretz—Gallery.*

Ze'evi, Rehavam. (1983/4). "The Master Plan for the Development of 'Haaretz Museum'" [in Hebrew]", *Israel—Am va-Aretz* A, 19: 247–64.

Zerubavel, Yael. (1995). *Recovered Roots: Collective Memory and the Making of the Israeli National Tradition.* 60–77. Chicago and London: University of Chicago Press.

Zusman, Ayala and Ronny Reich. (1987). "The History of the Rockefeller Museum" [in Hebrew]. In *Zev Vilnay's Jubilee* Volume 2. Edited by Ely Schiller. 83–92. Jerusalem, Ariel.

Personal Interviews

Abu-Raya, Amin. Director of the Arabic-Palestinian Heritage Museum, 17 June 2006.

Dabah, M. Rabbi of the Karaite synagogue, Jerusalem, 28 May 2008.

Dajani, Mahira. Director of the Arab Children's Home (telephone interview), 14 June 2008.

Gafni, Orit. Curator of the Italian Jewish Museum, 28 Aug. 2007.

Gozlan, Avraham. Director of the Worldwide North Africa Jewish Heritage Center, personal interview, Jerusalem, 31 Jan. 2007.

Halamish, Uzi. Director of the Joe Alon Center, 16 Aug. 2007.

Hon, Shuki. Director of the Circassian Heritage Museum, 30 January 2007.

Kesar, Yehiel. Director of the Association for Fostering society and Culture, Documentation and Research, 18 Nov. 2007.

Kohen, Yefet. Founder of the Samaritan Museum, Kiryat Luza, 27 Aug. 2008.

Lustig, Hava. Founder of The Memorial Museum of Hungarian Speaking Jewry, Safed, 30 January 2007.

Malachi, Zvi. Director of the Museum of Jewish Heritage in Israel, Lydda, 20 August 2007.

Mandler, Shimon. Director of the Treasures in the Wall Museum, Acre, 27 July 2008.

Mordechayov, Michael. Gabbai of the Tzerif (Hut) Synagogue for Bukharan Jewry, Kiryat Malachi, 17 Aug. 2008.

Mor-Hameiri, Yehudit. Director of Beit Hameiri, Safed, 21 Nov. 2007.

Nasaradin, Fadl. Druse Heritage House, Daliyat al-Karmel, 21 August 2007.

Pedazur, Avi. Director of the Museum of Libyan Jews, Or Yehuda, 20 Jun 2006.

Peretz, Eyal. Chairman of the The Turkish Community in Israel Association, Yehud, 20 Jun 2006.

Raimond, Reuven. Director of the Razei Gahelet Association, Beersheba, 16 Aug. 2007.

Shibli, Diyab. Director of the Bedouin Heritage Center, Shibli, 17 June 2006.

Thawcho, Zuheir. Founder of the Circassian Museum, Kafr Kama, 21 August 2007.

Internet Sites

Arkadaş —The Turkish Community in Israel Association: http://www.arkadas.org.il

Beit Hatfutsot: www.bh.org.il

Council for Conservation of Heritage Sites in Israel: http://www.shimur.org

Dapei Zahav (Yellow Pages): www.d.co.il

Education Ministry: http://education.gov.il

Eretz Israel Museum: www.eretzmuseum.org.il

Haaretz newspaper Archive: www.haaretz.co.il

ICOM – The International Council of Museums: http://icom.museum

Israel Museums Guide: www.ilmuseums.com

Knesset: http://knesset.gov.il

Libyan Jews Heritage Center: http://www.livluv.org.il

Memorial Museum of Hungarian Speaking Jewry: http://www.hjm.org.il/

Museum of Jewish Heritage in Israel: http://museum.zapages.co.il/

Revive the Family Association: http://www.inash.org/accomplishments/folklore.html

Shaar Zion Library Beit Ariela: http://ariela2.tau.ac.il/F

Treasures in the Wall: http://www.ozarot.net/

Museum Visiting Hours and Information

Museum Name	Address	Hours	Telephones	email/internet
Arab-Palestinian Museum of Culture and Heritage	Old City P.O.B. 1586 Sakhnin 30810	Mon–Thurs, Sat: 09:00–15:00	04-6746123 050-5457613	Email: sakhnin.museum@ hotmail.com
Babylonian (Iraqi) Jewry Heritage Museum	83 Mordechai Ben Porat Ave Or Yehuda	Sun-Mon, Wed-Thurs: 9:00–14:00 Tues: 9:00–17:00 Fri: 10:00-13:00	03-5339278/9 Fax: 03-5339936	Website: www.BabylonJewry.org.il Email: babylon@babylonjewry. org.il
Bedouin Heritage Center	P.O.B. 42 Kfar Shibli 16805	To be arranged in advance.	04-676 5585 Mobile: 052-279 2171 Fax: 04-677 2180	
Beit Hameiri Museum	158 Keren Hayesod St. Safed	Sun–Thurs: 08:00–14:30 Fri: 08:00–13:30	04-697 1307 04-692 1939	
Beit Hatfutsot— The Nahum Goldmann Museum of the Jewish People	Tel Aviv University Campus 15 Klausner St. Ramat Aviv Tel Aviv P.O.B. 39359 Tel Aviv 61392	Sun–Tues: 10:00–16:00 Wed–Thurs: 10:00–19:00 Fri: 09:00–13:00 Closed Sat and holidays	03-745-7808 Fax: 03-745 7811	Website: www.bh.org.il
Bukharan Jewry's "Mini-Museum"	Nahalat Habad St. Kiryat Malachi	To be arranged by telephone	Rabbi Michael Mordechayov 050-678 1822	
Plia Center, Bukharan Jewish Heritage Museum	36 Kziv St. Kfar Vradim	To be arranged by telephone	04-957 0752 Mobile: 050-6303231	Website: www.pliacenter.org/ Email: sahale@netvision.net.il
The Children of the Bible (Karaite Judaism) Heritage Museum	3 Tiferet Israel St. Jerusalem 97500	To be arranged by phone	02-627 4728 Mobile: 050-5733723 Fax: 02-627 4728	
Circassian Museum	P.O.B. 694 Kafr Kama 15235	Sun-Sat: 10:00-17:00	050-5857640	Website: http://www. shimur.org/Circassian Email: info@ circassianmuseum.co.il

Circassian Museum (The Circassian Experience— The Museum for the Preservation and Dissemination of Circassian Heritage) located in Rehaniya, Upper Galilee	The Circassian Experience Heritage in Rehaniya P.O.B. 24 Rehaniya 13818 Exp	Every day, Sun thru Saturday by advance arrangement	04–6980349 Mobile: 050-5203146 Fax: 04-698 7940	Website: www.adiga.co.il/
Cochin Jewish Heritage Center	Moshav Nevatim Doar Na HaNegev 85540	Sun–Thurs: 9:30–15:00	08-623 8299 Fax: 08-823 9575	Website: www.cochin.org.il/ Email: cochin11@walla.com
The Sheikh Nasradin Druze Heritage House	Daliyat al-Karmel Isfiya Center of the Commercial Market	To be arranged in advance	04-839 3242 Mobile: 052-344 3147 Fax: 04-839 7097	
Eretz Israel Museum	2 Haim Levanon Ramat Aviv Tel Aviv 69975	Mon–Wed: 10:00–16:00 Thurs: 10:00–20:00 (The Ethnography and Folklore Pavilion is open until 16:00) Sat: 10:00–14:00	03-641-5244	Email: mirit@eretzmuseum.org.il Website: www.eretzmuseum.org.il
The German-Speaking Jewry Heritage Museum	Tefen Industrial Park P.O.B. 1 Migdal Tefen 24959	Sun - closed Mon-Thurs: 09:00–16:00 Fri: 9:00–14:00 Sat: 10:00-16:00	04-910 9606 (Ruti Ofek)	Email: ruth@museum.org.il
The Memorial Museum of Hungarian Speaking Jewry	P.O.B. 1168 Safed		04-692 3880 Fax: 04-692 5881	Website: www.hjm.org.il

Israel Museum	11 Derech Ruppin Hakirya Jerusalem POB 71117 Jerusalem 91710	Sun, Mon, Wed, Thurs: 10:00–17:00 Tues: 16:00–21:00 Fri and Holiday eves: 10:00–14:00 Sat: 10:00–17:00	02-670-8855 02-670-8811	Email: info@imj.org.il Website: www. imjnet.org.il
The U. Nahon Italian Museum of Jewish Art	25 Hillel St. Jerusalem	Sun, Tues, Wed: 10:00–17:00 Thurs: 12:00–21:00 Fri: 10:00–13:00 Closed Monday and Saturday	02-624 1610 Fax: 02-625 3480	Email: info@heyraitalia.org Website: ijamuseum.org/he/
Joe Alon Center for Regional Studies	Joe Alon Center adjacent to Kibbutz Lahav D.N. Negev 85335	Sun–Thurs: 08:30-15:30	08-9913394	Website: www.joealon.org.il Email: office@joealon.org.il
The Museum of Jewish Heritage in Israel	20 Sderot Hamelech David Lod 71102	Sun–Thurs: 10:00–14:00 (Closed Fri and Sat)	08-924 4569 Mobile: 054- 446 4803 Fax: 08-924 9466	Website: museum.zapages.co.il/ Email: zmalachi@post.tau.ac.il
Museum of Libyan Jews	4 Moshe Hadadi St. Or Yehuda 60256	Sun–Thurs: 09:00–15:30	03-5336268/72 Fax: 03-533 3456	Email: luv@bezeqint.net Website: www.livluv.org.il
The Worldwide North Africa Jewish Heritage Center	13 HaMoghrabim St. Mahaneh Israel Neighborhood Jerusalem	Sun–Thurs: 08:00-15:00 Open only to groups, by advance arrangement	02-623 5811	Website: www.north-africa-jewish-heritage-center.org.il Email: merkazna@bezeqint.net
Old Yishuv Court Museum	6 Or haHayyim St. Jewish Quarter Jerusalem	March-November Sun—Thurs: 10:00–17:00 Fri–10:00–13:00 December-February Sun–Thurs: 10:00–15:00 Fri: 10:00–13:00 Hol haMo'ed Sukkot and Passover 10:00–18:00	02-627 6319 052-400 2478 Fax 02-6284636	Email: Museum-o@zahav.net.il Website: oymuseum.datinet.co.il/

Palestinian Heritage Center, Bethlehem	Manger St. P.O.B. 146 Bethlehem Palestine	Mon–Sat: 10:00–20:00	972 (or 970) 2-2742381 Fax: 972 (or 970) 2-2742642	Website: www.phc.ps/
Palestinian Heritage Museum of Dar el Tifl	Obaidah Ibn Jarrah St. East Jerusalem	Mon–Thurs, Sat: 8:00–16:00	02-627 2531 Fax: 02-6272341	
Samaritan Museum	Kiryat Luza, Mt. Gerizim, Nablus	Open all hours of the day Groups by advance arrangement with a Hebrew guide	053-886 2504 Guy	Email: shomron082@gmail.com
Turkish Jewry Heritage Center	15 Tannenbaum St. P.O.B. 7350 Yehud 56000	To be arranged in advance	03-536 1666 Fax: 03-5360447	Website: www.arkadas.org.il
Treasures in the Wall— Ethnography Center	2 Weizmann St. Acre	Sun-Thurs: 10:00–17:00 Fri: 10:00–16:00	04-991 1004 Fax: 04-9917059	Website: www.ozarot.net/
Wolfson Museum for Jewish Art–Hechal Shlomo	58 King George St. Jerusalem	Sun–Thurs: 09:00–15:00	02-5889000 Fax: 02-623 1810	Email: hechalshlomo@gmail.com Website: www.hechalshlomo.org.il
Museum for Yemenite Jewry Heritage of the Association for Society and Culture	11 Kikar haAtzma'ut Netanya	Sun-Thurs: 8:30–14:00	08-833 1325	Website: www.teman.org.il
Yemenite Jewish Heritage House	41 Shabazi Rosh Haayin 40800	Groups by advance arrangement	03-5034880/1 052-3575953 Fax: 03-938 4617	

Endnotes

1   Contrary to the common notion, Israel is not the country with the highest number of museums per person, nor is it even among the leading countries of the world in this respect. This statement appears from time to time in the name of various official elements; see, for example, Barzilai (2004, 62); also the information disseminated by the Ministry of Education on the occasion of the sixtieth anniversary of the foundation of the state (Administration of Society and Youth 2008, p. 6).

From the above data, in Israel there are at the most 30 museums per one million inhabitants. According to UNESCO publications, updated to 1998, in many western European countries there are over 40 museums for each million inhabitants. In Austria, 90 were listed and in Switzerland some 110 museums for every million residents. See also UNESCO (1998, section 10).

More current data are not available, since the organization stopped publishing them owing to difficulties in collecting information (in a personal communication with Ms Lydia Daloma of the UN Statistical Institute, Jan. 2008).

2   In distinction from artifacts excavated at archeological sites.

3   In general search engines as well as the Internet sites, Yellow Pages, www.d.co.il and Israel Museums Guide.

4   Mainly in the *Haaretz* archive and the computerized index of daily papers (edited by the Shaar Zion Library—Beit Ariela).

5   For the full list of museums, see page 208.

6   The muses are nine young goddesses in Greek mythology, each one in charge of maintaining and nurturing a certain art: epic poetry, music, love poetry, rhetoric, history, tragedy, comedy, dance, and astronomy.

7   This definition is valid today as well; noting, in addition, that the museum deals both with material and non-material heritage.

8   For example, quoted in this volume, among others, are studies by scholars in the field of sociology and anthropology (Deborah Fenichel and Kaylin Goldstein), communications (Tamar Katriel), culture (Ariella Azoulay), art (Yehudit Inbar), and education (Orna Yair). This current study was carried out within the Department of Geography of the Hebrew University of Jerusalem, in the field of historical geography.

9   As a result, national museums the world over are today seeking new ways to place "their" nation in its world context as well as confronting the problematic past of destructive, suppressive nationalism (for example, in Germany, South Africa, and Australia), and see Davison (2006).

10   In the period under discussion, the term "Palestine" did not constitute a defined political entity. In the nineteenth century, it was not usually referred to as a designated geographic unit, separate from its environment but rather as part of Syria. Thus, we must make clear that the term "Palestine" in this book refers to a region delimited during the British Mandate and in which the State of Israel was later established.

11   This museum still exists but it is open only for students of the school and invitees.

12   The structure still exists and serves today as a girls school.

13   Catalogue, in Turkish, printed in 1910 and kept to this day in the library of the Rockefeller Archeological Museum.

14   The museums in New York and Warsaw were founded on the basis of private collections and not as the result of public endeavor.

15   The importance of An-sky's contribution to the founding of Jewish ethnography is attested by two exhibitions devoted to him and his activity: an exhibition held at the Eretz Israel Museum in 1971 on the occasion of the fiftieth anniversary of his death and an exhibition mounted at the Israel Museum in 1994. See Davidovitch (1971) and Gonen (1994).

16   Until the end of the Ottoman period, in Eretz Israel there were at least 30 museums and collections.

17   See, for example, Kol-Inbar (1992, 2).

18   This was the first time the Citadel served in a non-security capacity.

19   To be sure, these activities held a prime place in the Zionist movement well before 1948, but with the founding of the State of Israel they were institutionalized and intensified immensely. Much has been published on this issue; see, for example, Shapira (1997), Naveh and Yogev (2002), and Zameret (1997).

20   On the recruitment of Israeli archeology for the benefit of Judaizing Eretz Israel space and on the place of the museums in this process, see, for example, Azoulay (1993); Abu El-Haj (1988); Kletter (2006).

21   The founding was financed mainly by donations from Jewish philanthropists and a support grant from the American government. The State of Israel is part owner of the museum, and it allots it financial support according to a generous

key relative to the other museums it aids. Some 42% of all government support for all the museums in the State of Israel goes to the Israel Museum, and this sum covers about 15% of the museum's current budget, which still depends mainly on contributions (Rapp 2005, 63).

22   The political pressure continued and ultimately, in 1979, in the Arts Wing a separate department for Israeli art was established. This division has continued to be the subject of controversy among the wing's curators to this day; see also Rapp (2005, 104).

23   Noy established the Ethnology Museum in Haifa and is considered the founder of the discipline of ethnology in Israel.

24   See the exhibition catalog (Muller-Lancet 1973); the success of the exhibition was also evident in the fact that in a rare move another edition of the catalog was published ten years later.

25   In the Bukharan Jewry exhibition, the first to be held in the Ethnography Department, still included were Judaica items that included inscriptions, such as a *parokhet* (Torah curtain) and *rimonim* (Torah finials); and see Muller-Lancet, Bukhara.

26   Muller-Lancet quoted by Fenichel 2005, 92).

27   In 2007, the permanent exhibition of the museum was closed for three years to allow wide-ranging refurbishment, and it may be that a result will be the unification of the two departments also with regard to display. On the renovation program for the museum, see, for example, Zandberg (2007, 11); Darom (2008).

28   While the first three were found in the previous exhibit, the Suriname synagogue was displayed for the first time with the opening of the refurbished museum in 2010.

29   On the Masada myth and its recruitment by the Zionist movement, see Zerubavel (1995).

30   Today, the Felicja Blumenthal Music Center is located there. The original building was razed in the 1990s.

31   According to the museum workers, its isolated location means that few visitors reach it.

32   To gain an impression of the appearance of the main display room, see the museum's Internet site at http://www.eretzmuseum.org.il/virtualtour/folklor.html

33   The information was obtained from workers in the registration department of the Haifa Museums, July 2008.

34   "Previous Exhibits" and "Catalogs," Internet site of Beit Hatfutsot: http://www.
      bh.org.il/Exhibitions/prevtemporary.asp

35   Statements by MK Amnon Cohen, Protocol #446 of the Knesset Economics
      Committee, 19 July 2005.

36   Statements by MK Amnon Cohen, Protocol #536 of the Knesset Economics
      Committee, 28 Nov. 2005.

37   In time, he told of one of the instances that made him come to this realization
      that had occurred in 1959, when he was active on the Netanya Workers
      Committee. That year, he was given the task of taking Yemenite immigrants
      who lived in a *ma'abara* (transit camp) to an opera performance in Tel Aviv.
      The new immigrants dressed in their traditional festive clothing ("their best
      shirts") and onto the four waiting buses they loaded blankets, *jaa'la* (a mixture
      of seeds and nuts), and liquor, "as if they were traveling to a real celebration."
      After these immigrants grew enthusiastic during the performance and clapped
      hands very loudly, they were removed from the concert hall; they spread their
      blankets on the seashore and had a Yemenite-style party all night long. The story
      is picturesquely related in Mizrahi (2000, 75–76).

38   In 1997, the association's name was changed, so today it is the Association for Fostering
      the Society and Culture of the Heritage of the Yemenite Jewry and the Tribes of Israel.

39   In one of the association's first publications, a letter by two young women from
      Jerusalem was quoted in which they apologized for not being able to attend
      its events held in Netanya and even expressed their wish "to receive letters
      from nice, tall young men, aged 28 to 35." This was followed by the editor's
      comment: "Bachelors with Initiative—Let's Go!" See (Ben-Shalom 1975, 7).

40   The term "Old Yishuv" was coined at the end of the nineteenth century by
      the first Zionists, and it denotes the entirety of the Jews who lived in Israel at
      that time and were not Zionists in distinction from the "New Yishuv," whose
      members belonged to the Zionist movement. The words "old" and "new" do
      not refer to chronological order but give expression to the ideological-value
      differences between the two groups. Today it is common to challenge the
      validity of these concepts, since the reality of life was not as dichotomous as this
      usage would seem to indicate. See, for example, Bartal (1976).

41   In its first ten years, over half a million visitors came to it. See Weingarten (1987).

42   One of the new kollelim was the *kollel* of Moghrabi Jews which broke off from
      the Sephardi *kollel.* For more on the splitting into factions that developed in the
      Yishuv in Jerusalem in the nineteenth century, see Eliav (1981, 136–139); Ben-
      Arieh (1977, 319–36).

43   This was a historical building erected at the end of the nineteenth century as the Schmidt School–a German Catholic institution that included a girls school, an orphanage, and a hostel for pilgrims. In 1910, the Catholic institution moved to the St. Paul hostel, a new building constructed for it opposite the Damascus Gate, where it still stands.

44   Saraf had already been active earlier among the Tunisian Jewish community and was one of the organizers of the national conference of Tunisian Jews in 1979; see M. Saraf (1979, 17).

45   For a more detailed description of the rooms and the many displayed items, see L. Mouchon (2007, 40–45).

46   http:/museum.dpages.co.il

47   On this campaign, see extensively in the autobiographical work Ben-Porat (1996).

48   Ben-Porat as quoted in Ben-Porat (1996).

49   The Babylonian exile numbered more than ten thousand people—all the members of the middle and upper classes in Judea, after the northern Kingdom of Israel had already been destroyed. The term "Babylonian Jewry" was used in the Land of Israel as early as the nineteenth century to distinguish between the homogeneous community in southern Iraq and the Jews of Kurdistan, who lived in the northern part of Iraq and constituted a socially and culturally distinct community (they consider themselves descendants of the Kingdom of Israel who had been exiled by the Assyrians). For historical evidence presenting both sides, see Yehuda (2002, 10–14).

50   As early as the master plan of 1970, it was planned that to be established on that site was a "folklore museum and an institute for research into the Holy Scriptures," and see Bar (1970, 17).

51   Despite this, Avishur attests that "in this instance, the presentation of items was made in an original manner since we did not copy any existing museum, neither in Israel nor abroad"; see also Avishur (1989, 6–8).

52   The center's bulletin even published an article praising the inclusion of the Farhud in the exhibit of the Los Angeles Museum of the Holocaust. See also "'The Farhud'—Part of the Holocaust" (2005, 39).

53   Contributions sent by Jews to support co-religionists in the Holy Land. It was divided by decision of the Jewish authorities in Jerusalem.

54   This was preceded by a number of structures that were built over the years outside the city walls by its Arab inhabitants; Christian public institutions, such

as Kerem Avraham, the Schneller institution, and the Russian Compound; as well as the first, and well known, Jewish neighborhood Mishkenot Sha'ananim, which was built by residents of the city at the initiative of an external element—Moses Montefiore; see also Ben-Arieh (1979, 93–119); for many years, it was thought that Nahalat Shiva was the first to be built by the Jews of Jerusalem even though Mahane Israel preceded it; see also Kark (1984, 20–21).

55   Another building in the neighborhood was renovated in 1993 and serves as the Gesher Center, today on 10 David Hamelech Street.

56   A few thousand remained in Libya, almost all of whom left as a result of riots in 1967, some to Israel and some to Italy, and see De Felice (1980, 253, 310–15).

57   See also statements by Pedazur in the Protocol of session no. 113 of the Knesset Absorption and Diaspora Affairs Committee, 27 Nov. 2000.

58   Internet site of the Libyan Jewry Heritage Center: http//www.livluv.org.il

59   One can see a slide show of pictures from the exhibit on the website of the Libyan Jewry Heritage Center at the address http://livluv.org.il/Index. asp?CategoryII)-123.

60   The preference of Libyan Jews to settle in agricultural settlements took on a main role in the self-image of the *edah*, and it is stressed in the writings of Libyan Jewry despite the fact that most of them actually live in cities. See, for example, Tzuriel (1960, 345–62).

61   For a broad description of Karaite theology and polemics between it and Rabbinic Judaism, see Elgamil (1979); for a concise description of differences in customs, see pages 19–22.

62   In Turkish, the word "arkadaş" means "friend."

63   The information was provided by different clubs and associations for people in Israel stemming from these communities.

64   According to a search of the Knesset legislation site http://knesset.gov.il/laws/heb/Law_Main.asp (accessed on 20 August 2008).

65   Statements by the lawyer Miriam Gerazi Rosenbaum, legal advisor to the Education Ministry, from Protocol 242 of the Education and Culture Committee meeting, 20 February 2001.

66   Statements by Edna Harel, legal adviser to the Ministry of Science, Culture, and Sport, from Protocol no. 1 of a meeting of the joint committee of Aliyah, Absorption, and Diaspora Affairs Committee and the Knesset Financial Committee on the topic of proposing a bill for the study of the heritage of Ethiopian Jewry, 5759-1999, 6 March 2001.

67   For example, statements by Dr. Zvi Zameret, director of the Ben-Zvi Institute, in Protocol no. 239 of the Knesset Education and Culture Committee, 11 June 2001.

68   Statements by Samir Wahba, the adviser to the prime minster on Druze affairs, and a successful contractor director of the Druze Department in Ministry of Science, Culture, and Sport, in Protocol no. 128 of the meeting of the Knesset Education, Culture, and Sport Committee, 29 January 2007.

69   The first museum was established in the Gaza Strip in 2008 by Jawwad al-Khoudry, but it is devoted solely to archeology and has no ethnographic exhibits. On the museum, see Bronner (25 July 2008).

70   Including efforts to obtain the return of archeological findings that Israeli institutions excavated in Palestine Authority territory; see, for example, M. Rappaport (11 April 2008).

71   Internet site of the Revive the Family organization: http://www.inash.org/accomplishments/folklore.html

72   From the museum brochure.

73   In 1995, the museum appeared in the museum guide published by Ariel; see also Inbar and Schiller (1995).

74   A theological debate surrounding this issue has been ongoing for some two thousand years—since the building of the Second Temple as described in Ezra 4; on the history of the Samaritan community and the debate over time, see extensively Stern and Eshel (2002).

75   On the budgetary problems, see "In Kiryat Luza Arrangements Are Beginning" (1993, 5); another museum was planned for the Samaritan neighborhood in Holon; see "Initial Steps Have Been Taken to Recruit Support for the Founding of a Museum of Samaritan Heritage in Holon," (1990, 4).

76   http//samaritans-mu.com

77   Hakohen is brimming with complaints against the officer of the Archeological Department of the Civil Administration, which carried out extensive archeological excavations on Mount Gerizim but is unwilling to provide items for the museum. Hakohen considers this theft of the Samaritan heritage. Moreover, physical access to the mountain has been blocked by the Archeology Authority, even though a visitors' center was built on site.

78   Yosef (Joe) Alon, a pilot, one of the founders of the Israel Air Force, a founder of the Hazerim base and its first commander, was murdered in the United States in 1973, when he was serving there as Israel's air attaché in Washington, D.C.

79   Halamish has said that it had previously been suggested to him to call the place "The National Museum for Bedouin Culture" and to stop delving into other subjects, but he was against the idea.

80   Treasures in the Wall, the museum website http://www.ozarot.net

81   Ibid.

82   On Ben-Zion Dinur as the national historian, see U. Ram (2006, 25–51); on the "leap" in Zionist historiography, which links the past to the present, see Y. Zerubavel (1995, 32–36).

83   The date 20 Tammuz is the anniversary of Herzl's death, which was a memorial day of the entire Zionist movement from 1904, the year of his death, until the establishment of the State of Israel. In 1948, it was even proposed to make it a national state holiday. It differs from the Herzl Day set in 2004 by the Knesset as 10 Iyyar, his birthday, so as to make it fall within the school year. On Herzl Day, see Azaryahu (1995, 20–24).

84   An echo of this is on the museum's Internet site, which states: "The horrific Holocaust destroyed this wonderful Judaism. Yet, the Holocaust of Hungarian Jewry did not receive the place it deserves in other museums." From the Internet site of the Memorial Museum of Hungarian Speaking Jewry, www.hjm.org.il, the page "About the exhibits."

85   Sometimes the museum is also called "The Museum for the Commemoration of Hungarian-Speaking Jewry," for example, in its official name in English, Memorial Museum for Hungarian Speaking Jewry.

86   On the stressing of valor in commemoration of the Holocaust, see, for example, Ben-Amos and Bet-El (1999, 470–71) and Brog (2003).

87   The Internet site of the Memorial Museum of Hungarian Speaking Jewry, www. hjm.org.il, the "Programs for Children and Youth" page.

88   During the Second World War, Libya was under Italian rule, and as a result the Libyan Jews suffered from the Italian racial laws; a few hundred of them were murdered in concentration camps in Libya and Europe.

89   The museum's Internet site http://www.hjm.org.il/EduProg.asp

90   See also Katriel (1997, 64).

91   As noted above, one of the criteria for receiving official recognition from the Education Ministry is that the museum be a not-for-profit institution.

92   From this list, the only recognized museums are the Joe Alon museum, the Old Yishuv Court Museum, the museum of Italian Jewry, and the Tefen museum. See the list of recognized museums in Rousso (2004, 20–21).

93   For example, Itzhak Katzenelson Holocaust and Jewish Resistance Heritage Museum, the Yad Mordechai Museum, Terezin House in kibbutz Givat Haim (Ihud), Chamber of the Holocaust on Mount Zion in Jerusalem, Masua Museum on kibbutz Tel Yitzhak, and Hannah Szenes House at kibbutz Sdot Yam.

94   Except for the museum in Sakhnin; see chapter 6, 4.d.

95   For details, see chapter 7.b and 7.c.

96   For example, in Azoulay (1993, 84).

97   Especially in the unofficial small museums and heritage centers, there is no catalogue or orderly registration of objects. All the information on the collection and on the items is in the heads of the museum founders, who also serve as guides to the visitors. In most of the museums the guidance is an obviously integral part of visiting the museum, and sometimes the museum is not open to the public except by appointment, and including tours guided by the museum staff.

98   On this community, which dwelled in three villages in the Ghariyan region and settled in Israel in moshav Porat in the Sharon, see the statements by Nahum Slouschz, quoted in Frija Zoaretz et al. *(1960, 39–40)*.

99   The Internet site of Arkadaş–The Turkish Community in Israel: http://www.arkadas.org.il/index/center/about_h.htm

100 Some of them are no longer active, at least on a regular basis.

101 The museum's Internet site: http://www.hjm.org.il/

102 For example, today the museum contains objects contributed by immigrants from the Former Soviet Union who fought in the Red Army, and it holds cultural evenings especially for elderly immigrants.

103 For example, *Nehardea* published by the Babylonian Jewish Heritage Center, *Kol ha-Italkim* published by the Museum of Italian Jewry, *Arkadaş* published by the Turkish Jewry Heritage Center, and *Kesharim* published by the Libyan Jews organization.

104 For examples, see the list of references at the end of the book.

105 "The Association's Aims," the association's Internet site, http://www.arkadas.org.il

106 Some of them are no longer operative today, at least not on a regular basis.

107 Marahti—a spoken language in western India and used by the "Bene Israel" community from India.

108 Adnan Farajallah, quoted in Stein (1998, 107).